The Nation's
Favourite Hymns

Remembering with affection
Stewart Cross (1928–89),
bishop of the Church of England
and director of *Songs of Praise*.

Songs of Praise
The Nation's Favourite Hymns

ANDREW BARR

A LION BOOK

Copyright © 2002 Andrew Barr
This edition copyright © 2002 Lion Publishing

The author asserts the moral right
to be identified as the author of this work

Published by
Lion Publishing plc
Mayfield House, 256 Banbury Road,
Oxford OX2 7DH, England
www.lion-publishing.co.uk
ISBN 0 7459 5118 X

By arrangement with the BBC

The BBC logo and the *Songs of Praise* logo are trade
marks of the British Broadcasting Corporation and
are used under licence

BBC logo © BBC 1996
Songs of Praise logo © BBC 2000

First edition 2002
10 9 8 7 6 5 4 3 2 1 0

A catalogue record for this book is available
from the British Library

Typeset in 9/12 Modern 880

Printed and bound in Singapore

Contents

Foreword

In his magical essay *Hymns in Man's Life*, D.H. Lawrence wonders at the undying power of hymns learned in childhood. The words become friends. They never leave us.

That is certainly my experience, and I am honoured to write this foreword for *The Nation's Favourite Hymns*. As a boy, I served as an organist in several churches and chapels in my native South Wales. Hymns are the richest part of worship there. There was a time when I could identify virtually any hymn or tune by its number in the *Methodist Hymn Book*! Age, alas, is taking its toll now.

In short, I love hymns. They can be powerful and gentle, uplifting and reassuring, intimate and inclusive. They are a gloriously simple way of communicating with God. They are also valuable signposts as we stumble on the pathways of faith.

There are times in life when each of us has cause to seek the 'still small voice of calm' of which John Greenleaf Whittier wrote so beautifully in 'Dear Lord and Father of mankind'. This is without doubt my top hymn. It is about celebration, praise, lifelong faith and God's guidance. We had no hesitation in choosing it for our wedding:

And let our ordered lives confess
  the beauty of thy peace.

It would be astonishing if the order and contents of this volume provoked no disagreement. I am happy to say that I disagree with parts of it. That's the fun of choosing any kind of list! My top ten would certainly include 'Now thank we all our God' (sung to the majestic 'Nun Danket'), but it would also feature the Easter hymn 'Jesus Christ is risen today, Alleluia!' (paired with the powerful Welsh tune 'Llanfair' by Robert Williams). The latter brings back happy childhood memories of the great Easter meetings held in one of the splendid chapels of Llanelli.

I hope you agree this is a magnificent collection. Enjoy!

HUW EDWARDS
Presenter, *BBC 6 O'Clock News*

Acknowledgments

Many people have helped me in the writing of this book. Apart from the hymn-writers and broadcasters named in the text, I am especially grateful to many friends and former colleagues in BBC Religion who continue an eighty-year-old tradition, bringing skill and enthusiasm to the task of broadcasting hymns and worship songs on *Songs of Praise*.

Michael Wood and Ian Hooker, musicians and musicologists, offered invaluable insights, as did the Reverend Johnston McKay.

Thank you to Kathleen Frew for converting my illegible hieroglyphics into a professional document, and my heartfelt gratitude to my wife Liz, herself a former religious programme maker, whose insights and criticisms as ever transform my work.

Morag Reeve, Jenni Dutton and Nick Rous, editor, copy-editor and designer respectively for Lion Publishing, have been patient and helpful as the text has expanded to try to do justice to all the facts, stories and experiences that make hymns matter to so many people, even if they do not go to church.

In George A. Birmingham's classic 'whodunnit', *The Hymn-Tune Mystery*, the crime is solved by John Dennis, cathedral precentor, who has an encyclopedic knowledge of hymns and hymn tunes, and finds the vital clue to who murdered Cresswood, the cathedral organist, in a code hidden in the notes of the tune for 'Jerusalem, my happy home'. I am all too aware of the many sleuths who have done their detective work on the legends that surround many of the writers of the nation's favourite hymns. Every theory is held with passion, and error in telling the story as it really was is high in the order of sins that cry to heaven for vengeance. I ask the reader's forgiveness for any mistakes I may have inadvertently made here. I hope that some of the stories and insights I have uncovered will add to the continuing story of *Songs of Praise*.

ANDREW BARR
Easter 2002

Prologue
From Here to Eternity

The countryside of Midlothian has disappeared under a blanket of snow by the time we have assembled in the medieval church for the funeral and begun singing the first hymn.

It is New Year's Eve, and I am singing 'Love divine, all loves excelling' surrounded by friends and neighbours, our breath making clouds in the cold air. There is no choir, but the organist leads us, and a sense of togetherness combined with the natural acoustic of a lofty chancel helps us believe that we really all sing rather well. Even in this Scots kirk, the moving words of an English hymn sung to the powerful Welsh tune 'Blaenwern' are helping us too, as we say goodbye to an old friend.

On a wet summer's day, the last day of August 1997, millions of viewers watching *Songs of Praise* also found solace together in Charles Wesley's words and the great Welsh tune. Diana, Princess of Wales, had died in a car crash in Paris the night before and we were all in shock. By early next evening, a special *Songs of Praise* was being broadcast live from St Paul's Cathedral, 'the nation's parish church' as presenter Pam Rhodes called it. The BBC news editor had cameras positioned at RAF Northolt, waiting for the moment when the Princess's body was flown back home. In an unprecedented cooperation between news and religious broadcasters, just as thousands of people began to sing 'Love divine, all loves excelling' in the cathedral, the *Songs of Praise* director showed us the BBC Newsroom's sombre pictures of the aircraft flying in under a grey sky, and the RAF bearer party carrying the flag-draped coffin across the tarmac. These sad images combined with the sound and words of a hymn caught the mood of the nation.

Ever since I first squawked my way through Jane Leeson's children's hymn, 'Loving shepherd of thy sheep', during a brief appearance in the Sunday school of Beckenham Congregational Church, I have been hooked on hymns. Whenever I hear 'Loving shepherd of thy sheep' sung to the tune 'Buckland' (which is all too rarely on *Songs of Praise* these days), memories of an airless room, where fidgeting small boys were corralled with tall, athletic girls, come rushing back.

But the charm of the hymns we sang together grabbed me then and grabs me still.

My next memory is of the small memorial chapel of Rugby School, where Bobby Broxton, an old chaplain in the Studdert-Kennedy mould, in teaching us to sing 'All things bright and beautiful', somehow conveyed to me that every blade of grass is a miracle. Formal creeds and catechisms have passed me by, but theology has come to me almost by osmosis as hymns and songs have lodged in my mind – a process that has been greatly helped by more than thirty years producing *Songs of Praise*.

Sometimes it is a new composition, like Peter Skellern's hymn, 'Rest in peace and rise in glory', written in 2001 for a Remembrance Sunday programme from York Minster, that I cannot get out of my head. Sometimes I gain a fresh understanding of an old hymn. In 1987, while I was visiting a remote part of Sri Lanka, where civil war had become a way of life, a young woman from the island's tiny Anglican community began to sing 'The Old Rugged Cross'. She was unaccompanied and quite alone. She sang each verse from memory and from the heart. It no longer sounded like the sentimental old potboiler derided by most church musicians, but a defiant cry of faith, the song of a woman surviving in a violent, male-dominated world. The strange, reedy sound of her voice rising above the high murmur of tropical birds still travels with me.

My other great enthusiasm, apart from hymns, is for the railway. In 1845, an anonymous writer signing himself as 'A Spiritual Watchman of the Church of England' claimed to have uncovered the ultimate source of lust and pride: 'It is to be found in the railway... we believe it is the masterpiece of Satan.'

A railway journey on the 05.55 a.m. departure from

Edinburgh to London is a sin I am happy to indulge in, as the world gradually wakes up on our way south. It is a journey from darkness to light. On an ordinary winter's weekday morning, the bleary-eyed dawn traveller peers out to the east, attracted by the silver shine on the North Sea, calm after an overnight storm. In the foreground, against a flat, pale sky, the hills of the border region are smooth undulations, topped by rank upon rank of gnarled, bare branches. We could be travelling through one of the pent-up landscapes of the nineteenth-century visionary painter, Samuel Palmer.

As the hills part near St Abb's Head, you get a glimpse of the tiny harbour of Burnmouth. A fishing boat, dark but for the bright pinpoints of its red and green navigation lights, is almost home. Otherwise, the world seems empty, waiting for another day of human invasions. The grey dawn light illuminates the green hills of Britain that inspired the famous Good Friday hymn of Cecil Frances Alexander, the Victorian hymn-writer. But it is an old Baptist hymn that runs round my head:

The light of the morning is breaking,
  the shadows are passing away;
the nations of earth are awaking,
  new peoples are learning to pray.

The faraway black lump across the sea is Holy Island, where the Northumbrian St Cuthbert prayed the Passion, reliving the violent and revolting events of first-century Palestine as a man died in agony on a hillside above Jerusalem.

Let wrong, great Redeemer, be righted,
  in knowing and doing your will;
and gather, one family united,
  the whole world to your cross on the hill.

Just before Berwick-upon-Tweed, thin bands of cloud on the horizon turn pink. Here, enemy battle cruisers once hovered at another daybreak on the North Sea. In 1914, their surprise bombardment was the first intimation for the people living along Britain's east coast that the most terrible war of the twentieth century had begun in earnest. Cyril Musgrove, organist of St Martin's, Scarborough, was playing the opening hymn for early communion when two German shells struck the building. Next morning, newspapers reported the outrage that churches had been the particular target of the enemy.

On my own journey, a peaceful, natural heat is

brewing. In less than a minute, the brilliant red disc of the sun rises above the horizon, and for just a few moments, it is safe to look straight at it.

Though hills and high mountains should tremble,
  though all that is seen melt away,
your voice shall in triumph assemble
  your loved ones at dawning of day.

Minutes later, there is full daylight, and the train has become bright and noisy. As we cross into England, mobile phones are ringing. The 'real' world has taken over.

We live surrounded by noise and music. But sometimes, through hymns, the sacred surprises our secular world. A hymn tune played on the bagpipes appeared on *Top of the Pops* during the late 1970s, when the pipe band of the Royal Scots Greys performed 'Amazing Grace'. 'The whole planet knows "Amazing Grace",' says popstar Toyah Wilcox. A television congregation on *Dial a Hymn* sang 'Glory be to God on high' to the signature tune from *EastEnders*. One producer even has the *Songs of Praise* title music as a ringtone on his mobile phone.

A hymn was used to haunting effect in Alberto Cavalcanti's war-propaganda film of the 1940s, *Men of the Lightship*. An old seaman picks out the tune for 'Lead, kindly light' on his squeeze box as his wartime lightship in the North Sea is threatened by enemy attack. His colleague says, 'I wish you'd find another tune – let's have a change!' and switches on the radio. 'I don't know any other tune,' says the old sailor. On the radio, an orchestra is playing the same tune. 'The beam of the lightship shines through the darkness to reach all who need it,' says the commentator. And at the end, the message of the film is underlined by the same voice: 'The Nazis must be stopped. We can and we will stop them.' The huge popularity of this film with wartime audiences was because something more profound than mere propaganda had been communicated. It was John Henry Newman's old hymn that carried the film's deeper message of hope through sacrifice.

What makes a hymn memorable? Why are some hymns like theological ticking time bombs, buried deep in the mind, ready to suddenly awaken a new understanding of faith? It is often at a funeral that a hymn suddenly strikes a deep chord and becomes a favourite. 'This need not be a bad thing,' says Ian Mackenzie, minister, musician and religious programme maker. 'There are thrills about playing the organ for hymn-singing at a funeral. Although there's no choir, there are often a lot of people there, and almost certainly 100 per cent more men than in a Sunday congregation. They produce a full-throated sound, dramatic and theatrical, almost like a Verdi opera chorus. The funeral is an event which is tremendously and deeply real for everyone present, and hymns play a huge part in this.'

Roger Royle, presenter of Radio 2's *Sunday Half-Hour*, agrees with Ian about the place of hymns at a funeral. 'My favourite hymn is "Just as I am", which I'm going to have for my funeral, so I hope people are practising now!'

Tom Jones, who has broadcast with Sir Harry Secombe, says that his colleagues in the Cwmbach Male Choir, which once famously sang with Paul Robeson, always gather at the 'Crem.' to sing 'Love divine, all loves excelling' when a member dies. Jones is not a native Welsh speaker, but says he feels that he especially understands a hymn when he sings it in Welsh. The choir, based in Aberdare, travels the world with a huge international repertoire – but singing Welsh hymn tunes is a part of their being.

So, what makes a hymn popular? What has made the forty hymns in this book stand out from the thousands of other hymns and worship songs that are sung in churches and on television and radio every week? Does the list change, and are the hymns all the ones you would expect?

For the last twenty years, *Songs of Praise* viewers have been asked to choose their favourites. 'I can tell you which one will come out top,' said a Church of England bishop once, as I was planning a new TV series on favourite hymns. 'I'll bet you a fiver it'll be "Abide with me".' He lost his bet then, and he still loses it in the latest *Songs of Praise* top forty, where it only reaches number fourteen.

Long before *Songs of Praise* began, the musicologist Erik Routley was researching and analysing the hymns most frequently sung in BBC broadcasts in the 1950s, and in weekly services in Westminster Abbey. 'The day thou gavest, Lord, is ended' appeared on his 'favourites' list regularly in 1914, but had vanished by 1931. It was nowhere near the top on the radio in the 1950s, and 'Abide with me' was not sung at all in any of the services that were broadcast during that decade.

Today's number-one favourite hymn, as it has been for a decade, is 'How Great Thou Art' ('O Lord my God, when I in awesome wonder'). It first became known through Billy Graham's visits to Britain, and has continued to grow in popularity ever since, even though Graham's last major tour was in 1984. Not far behind, at number four, is another hymn popularised by Billy Graham, 'Great is thy faithfulness, O God my Father', which in the 1950s caused tube trains on London's Piccadilly Line to rock and roll as huge swaying crowds sang the hymn on their way home from Harringay Arena, where Graham was speaking.

Number two in the top forty, 'Dear Lord and Father of mankind', seems to touch a deep chord at those moments when we feel overwhelmed by bad news. The first-hand experience of sailing across Lake Galilee during a pilgrimage to Israel Palestine has made the hymn an obvious choice for many *Songs of Praise* viewers. The first verse asks for forgiveness in our own lives, and the hymn ends with a prayer for universal peace. After any religious broadcast on the theme of forgiveness that includes this hymn, producers have to be ready for an avalanche of letters, emails and telephone calls from the audience. As Hugh Faupel, the current editor of *Songs of Praise*, says, 'Hymns give a vocabulary to things we otherwise find great difficulty in expressing.'

At number three is 'The day thou gavest, Lord, is ended' – the hymn Queen Victoria chose for her diamond jubilee. She is reported not to have approved of the boisterous, emotional choruses of the evangelists Dwight L. Moody and Ira D. Sankey, which were also fashionable at the time, believing that their popularity would not last. More than a century later, both her own choice of jubilee hymn and the American revivalist hymns of Moody and Sankey are still hugely popular.

But not all the hymns in the top forty are 'old favourites'. Not far behind the top three are two Graham Kendrick hymns, plus two others written within the last twenty years. Also, the worship song 'My Jesus, my Saviour' is rising rapidly in the nation's affection and looks set for a place.

I have come to the end of my train journey from Edinburgh to London, and after months of researching the nation's favourite hymns, I celebrate the completion of my task at a midweek evensong at St Martin-in-the-Fields, Trafalgar Square. A choir sings the service, and a congregation of fewer than a dozen stands to join in singing a hymn. There is constant chattering and banging from the tramps, the homeless and the disturbed people who sit around the walls of the church. For half an hour or so, we are in their home, and the mêlée of sounds of the stories they mutter underneath the beautifully soaring harmonies of the small choir becomes itself like a spontaneous *Songs of Praise*. For, in the spirit of Dick Sheppard, the famous radio parson through whose pioneering services on steam radio the BBC first broadcast hymns in the 1920s, the church of St-Martin-in-the-Fields is always open to all.

The *Songs of Praise* production team still brings fresh hymns to the series, and soon there will be new favourites for the thousands of singers who are ready to help make this unique programme. The poet Alfred Noyes wrote some verse in the 1920s to commemorate the completion of what was then the largest and newest BBC transmitter at Daventry. He was inspired not only by it being built on a hill, sharing the site of a Saxon burial place, but also by the pioneering work of the producers and technicians who first had the ambition now shared by the team planning next year's *Songs of Praise*:

You shall hear their lightest tone
stealing through your walls of stone.

Till your loneliest valleys hear
the far cathedral's whispered prayer.

Daventry calling... Daventry calling... Daventry
calling... dark and still... the tree of memory stands
like a sentry... over the graves on the silent hill.

Note
As the popularity of hymns waxes and wanes, this book takes them in alphabetical order, but their position in the top forty of 2002 is included below each title.

Abide with me; fast falls the eventide

Words by Henry Francis Lyte (1793–1847)

Tune: 'Eventide' by William Henry Monk (1823–89)

This is a good hymn with which to begin the story of the nation's most popular hymns. 'A hymn, to be successful,' wrote the revivalist preacher Charles Haddon Spurgeon, 'should be more lovable than good poetry.' Henry Francis Lyte, the writer of 'Abide with me; fast falls the eventide', has succeeded in creating something that is both lovable *and* good poetry. The hymn has words and a tune that are picked up by football crowds without a hymn book in sight.

People have so many different pictures in their minds when they hear 'Abide with me'. They may be of choirboys in a Remembrance Sunday *Songs of Praise* at York Minster, or old grainy footage of the cup-final crowds at Wembley; a colliery band at sunset, or a graveyard. They might even be of the last dawn of nurse Edith Cavell's life, before she was shot for being a spy by the Germans in the First World War. The closing words of the hymn were the last she ever spoke.

Statue of Edith Cavell.

The story goes that neither words nor tune took more than a few minutes to write. William Henry Monk, the Victorian London organist, wrote the tune 'Eventide' in ten minutes. Such high-speed composition is an experience frequently described by hymn-writers, old and new, and I find it mysterious that so many of our profoundest and best-loved hymns are claimed to have been written in these sudden flashes of inspiration.

Lyte was born in 1793 at Ednam, near Kelso, in the Scottish borders. He was educated in Ireland, where he won poetry prizes. At first, he intended to be a doctor, but by the time he was twenty-one, he had become an Anglican priest. It seems, from a verse later omitted from 'Abide

with me', that at that time he still had some way to go in following the straight and narrow path:

Thou on my head in early youth didst smile.
And, though rebellious and perverse meanwhile,
thou hast not left, oft as I left thee.

The young clergyman, in his first charge in Ireland, sat with a neighbouring priest who was dying. The priest was in great mental distress because he could no longer believe in the eternal love of God. While reading for his friend the priest the account in Luke's Gospel of two travellers meeting the risen Jesus on the road to

---

Abide with me; fast falls the eventide;
the darkness deepens; Lord, with me abide,
when other helpers fail, and comforts flee,
help of the helpless, O abide with me.

Swift to its close ebbs out life's little day;
earth's joys grow dim, its glories pass away;
change and decay in all around I see;
O thou who changest not, abide with me.

I need thy presence every passing hour;
what but thy grace can foil the tempter's power?
Who like thyself my guide and stay can be?
Through cloud and sunshine, O abide with me.

I fear no foe, with thee at hand to bless;
ills have no weight, and tears no bitterness.
Where is death's sting? where, grave, thy victory?
I triumph still, if thou abide with me.

Hold thou thy cross before my closing eyes;
shine through the gloom, and point me to the skies;
heaven's morning breaks, and earth's vain shadows flee;
in life, in death, O Lord, abide with me.

Emmaus – a story that Lyte had read many times – Lyte suddenly found new meaning in it. From then on, although his own physical health began to fail, Lyte felt spiritually liberated.

He later moved to the Devonshire fishing port of Brixham, where he held the post of 'perpetual' curate, working tirelessly for the poor, and in support of the movement to abolish the slave trade. Whether Lyte wrote 'Abide with me' while in Ireland with his dying friend, or, as legend has it, years later after tea on the last Sunday that he preached in Brixham before his own death, we may never know. The image is archetypal: the worn-out old man, fighting off asthma, sitting on the rocks in the evening sunlight and looking at the famous Brixham trawlers lying peacefully at anchor, the fishing fleet in port. It could be a film sequence from any one of a hundred *Songs of Praise* programmes, and it perhaps describes the scene as Lyte wrote the final verse of a hymn that may have started in his mind in Ireland, many years earlier. Whatever the truth, it is a hymn that is first and last about death.

In 1978, Bill Nicholson, a young TV director who later was to have huge success with *Shadowlands*, a play about C.S. Lewis, tried to depict 'Abide with me' through a documentary film of 1970s' Britain. Full of nostalgia, the film illustrated the line 'change and decay in all around I see' with shots of a colliery brass band playing the hymn tune on top of a slag heap. Unfortunately, this line seems to have been embraced by some Christians as a reason for refusing to allow any change at all in their churches or in their lives. I am grateful to a Church of Scotland minister and friend who claims that what Lyte originally wrote was 'change, or decay, in all around I see' – which has rather the opposite meaning.

At a *Songs of Praise* recording in the Royal Concert Hall, Glasgow, in the 1990s, the late Cardinal Winning arrived at the end of an exhausting day. As he entered the auditorium, a huge choir was rehearsing, unaccompanied and in full harmony, the verse beginning 'Hold thou thy cross before my closing eyes'. He stopped so suddenly that his colleagues, who were behind him, ran into him. 'Listen,' he said to them. 'How are they managing that beautiful sound? It's the best ever.'

13

All things bright and beautiful

Words by Cecil Frances Alexander (1818–95)

Tunes: 'All Things Bright' by William Henry Monk (1823–1889); 'Royal Oak' by Martin Shaw (1875–1958)

Cecil Frances Humphreys grew up in nineteenth-century rural Ireland in a strict, evangelical household. When she was twenty-five, she produced a series of hymns for the children at her Sunday-school class, to help them learn their catechism. Not surprisingly, she married a clergyman, but although her husband was later to become an archbishop, the name Alexander is far better known as belonging to the author of some of the most famous Victorian hymns. Cecil Frances Alexander has bequeathed us 'Once in royal David's city', which was not originally meant as a Christmas carol, but to help children understand the Apostles' Creed, and 'There is a green hill far away'.

She wrote 'All things bright and beautiful' to help her young pupils – children growing up in the gentle, sylvan countryside of County Tyrone – to understand the opening words of the Apostles' Creed. 'Mrs Alexander has laid aside her theology and lost herself in the beauty of nature,' complained one preacher.

Mrs Alexander had a strong social conscience, and she worked tirelessly for the relief of the poor. But she talked little about the inner strength she found from her faith. Many of her hymns, inspired by what she

All things bright and beautiful,
all creatures great and small,
all things wise and wonderful,
the Lord God made them all.

Each little flower that opens,
each little bird that sings,
he made their glowing colours,
he made their tiny wings.

The purple-headed mountain,
the river running by,
the sunset, and the morning
that brightens up the sky:

The cold wind in the winter,
the pleasant summer sun,
the ripe fruits in the garden,
he made them every one.

He gave us eyes to see them,
and lips that we might tell
how great is God almighty,
who has made all things well.

saw around her, provide a glimpse of life in Ireland in the mid-nineteenth century. Unfortunately, 'All things bright and beautiful', which has cheered on so many rural, harvest and child-centred editions of *Songs of Praise*, originally contained a verse that is today regarded as a wildly politically incorrect:

The rich man in his castle,
  the poor man at his gate,
God made them, high or lowly,
  and ordered their estate.

Although long deleted from hymn books, the verse is still brought out like an ancient blunderbuss by critics of the church.

Erik Routley, the great historian of hymnody, enjoyed pointing out a verse in the original *Hymns Ancient and Modern* that regularly raised a laugh. It was from another of Mrs Alexander's hymns that drew on a local scene: walking with the children through the graveyard to church. It concludes with the lines:

They do not hear when the great bell
  is ringing overhead;
they cannot rise and come to church
  with us, for they are dead.

As Routley pointed out, Mrs Alexander did not intend such bald naivety, but was, as always, trying to answer the difficult and direct questions she was asked by the children.

When the BBC first broadcast hymns in the 1920s, *Radio Times* carried articles about the best known as they were transmitted. Amazingly, a reviewer of children's hymns suggested that Mrs Alexander's hymns were 'obscure'. There was more liking at that time for 'Little drops of water', a hymn written around the same time as 'All things bright and beautiful' by another Sunday-school teacher, Julia Carney, and now almost forgotten. This is indeed a very simple hymn about creation:

Little drops of water,
  little grains of sand,
make the mighty ocean,
  and the beauteous land.

Top marks were accorded to Arabella Hankey, another Victorian Sunday-school teacher, who wrote 'Tell me the old, old story', originally a poem of no fewer than fifty verses. It was made hugely popular by Moody and Sankey, using their recipe for success: a cheerful tune with an easily remembered chorus to tell a tough story. However, unlike 'All things bright and beautiful', it has hardly ever been requested in the twenty-five years since *Songs of Praise* introduced interviews.

Nigel Swinford, regular contributor to Radio 4's *Daily Service* and conductor for *Songs of Praise*, admires children's hymns that tell a good story, rather than those that dwell on sentimental memories of childhood. He points out that 'Tell me the old, old story' was originally written for children, but only took off when adults got to know it. The same can be said of Mrs Alexander's *Hymns for Little Children*.

Today, 'All things bright and beautiful' fits in with the ecological concerns of both adults and children. One *Songs of Praise* viewer says that she and her son regularly sing it to one another on the telephone. Although William Henry Monk's old tune and Martin Shaw's arrangement, 'Royal Oak', are still popular, a more recent tune by John Rutter has assured Mrs Alexander's hymn a new lease of life.

Amazing grace! how sweet the sound

(AMAZING GRACE)

Verses 1–6 by John Newton (1725–1807); verse 7 anonymous

Tune: 'Amazing Grace' (American traditional melody)

32

Amazing grace! how sweet the sound
  that saved a wretch like me;
I once was lost, but now am found,
  was blind, but now I see.

'Twas grace that taught my heart to fear,
  and grace my fears relieved;
how precious did that grace appear,
  the hour I first believed!

Through many dangers, toils and snares
  I have already come:
'tis grace that brought me safe thus far,
  and grace will lead me home.

The Lord has promised good to me,
  his word my hope secures;
he will my shield and portion be
  as long as life endures.

Yes, when this heart and flesh shall fail,
  and mortal life shall cease,
I shall possess within the veil
  a life of joy and peace.

The earth shall soon dissolve like snow,
  the sun forbear to shine,
but God, who called me here below,
  will be for ever mine.

When we've been there a thousand years,
  bright shining as the sun,
we've no less days to sing God's praise
  than when we first begun.

'A year ago, I was in the gutter, screaming to die. It just wasn't a life, I was desperate.' In a quiet house in the west end of Glasgow, Dave is describing drug addiction. *Songs of Praise* cameras have come to hear his story as a prelude to a hymn that so closely reflects his experience.

With the help of new friends in a Church of Scotland rehabilitation centre, Dave is on the long, painful journey away from his drug habit. 'We couldn'ae do it ourselves. Being here gives you a sense of belonging. For the first time, we're with people who come up and hug us and say we're all right; we're used to just being pushed away. Now I can pray; I've found faith and it's given me a result.'

As Dave tells his story, the simple notes of a tune played on a solitary pipe can be heard, heralding a huge choir singing, 'Through many dangers, toils and snares I have already come.'

The unfussy harmony singing that night would have gladdened the heart of John Newton, the hymnwriter whose autobiography is revealed in 'Amazing Grace'. It seems he thought that any music other than hymns was the 'exclusive prerogative of Satan', and in 1748, he chastised Handel for his *Messiah* 'which turned scripture into entertainment'.

The story of Newton, captain of an African slave ship, gradually turning to a new life, is familiar to *Songs of Praise* and *Sunday Half-Hour* audiences. 'I often petitioned that the Lord would be pleased to fix me in a more humane calling,' he said.

Newton, who had followed his father to sea at the age of eleven, was always studious. He learned Euclidean mathematics and taught himself Latin while surviving the violent world of eighteenth-century seafaring. Because he was self-taught and had not been to university, he was at first rejected for ordination by the Church of England. The Archbishop of York said he would be a fool to give up a good worldly position for an uncertain career as a clergyman. 'What a farce!' noted John Wesley in his journal, after he had met Newton.

Finally, Newton's persistence was rewarded and he was ordained. He was fortunate in meeting one of the great 'lights' of the Calvinistic revival, the poet and hymn-writer William Cowper, who wrote 'O for a closer walk with God' and 'God moves in a mysterious way'. Newton encouraged his poet neighbour to cope with terrible depression by writing hymns, and together in 1779 they produced the *Olney Hymns*, named after the Buckinghamshire parish where Newton was curate. Both Newton and Cowper wrote from a personal experience of faith, which came less as a Damascus road encounter and more as a gradual change of heart. Right up to his death, Newton spoke not of the darkness, but of the marvel in his life. Providence had intervened. 'I am a great sinner,' he said, 'but Jesus Christ is a great Saviour.'

In the pulpit, he was not a great preacher. Towards the end of his life, as vicar of St Mary Woolnoth, in London, he muttered and mumbled, but people still flocked to see him. He refused to retire. 'What?' he said. 'Shall the old African blasphemer stop while he can speak?'

African slave convoy on its way to a slave ship. Early-nineteenth-century copperplate engraving.

The gospel singer Gloria Gaynor, America's 'queen of disco' during the 1970s and 1980s, sang 'Amazing Grace' at the fortieth-birthday gala *Songs of Praise* in London's Royal Albert Hall. She described Newton's words as 'wonderful and heartfelt and about my first love, which is Christ. She told presenter Aled Jones, 'These words make me feel honoured and yet humble. They give credence and purpose to my life.'

The singer has herself experienced a long and difficult journey of conversion, turning from 'sex, drugs and disco' to become a deeply committed 'born-again' member of her gospel church in Brooklyn. 'What's your recipe?' asked Jones. She summed it up in her inimitable

John Newton.

style: 'Find out what God's doing, and get in on it!'

Back in Glasgow, as Dave found faith to cope with his addiction, he said, 'Somebody told me that religion was for people who don't want to go to hell; I discovered that spirituality is for people who've been there.'

And can it be that I should gain

Words by Charles Wesley (1707–88)

Tune: 'Sagina' by Thomas Campbell (1825–76)

12

On 24 May 1738, the Princess of Wales gave birth to a son at her home in St James's Square, London. The baby, who was immediately christened George, was destined to be King George III.

On the same day, a young curate attended a service in the new St Paul's Cathedral, rebuilt after the great fire of London in 1666 had reduced it to ashes, its brilliant white stone standing out above the murky city skyline. There, he heard the choir sing William Croft's setting of Psalm 130, beginning with the solo, 'Out of the deep have I called unto thee O Lord; O Lord, hear my voice.' Nowadays, with regular broadcasts from St Paul's, including *Songs of Praise*, we can all imagine the almost mystical feeling he must have experienced as the sound floated through London's greatest building to the congregation.

But as John Wesley, that same curate, records, what followed at a Bible meeting 'at a quarter before nine that same evening', was far more mysterious. Recalling the words of the psalm, 'O Lord, hear my voice,' he suddenly felt 'strangely warmed'. It was a moment of personal conversion that was to influence

Charles Wesley.

the course of Christianity around the world. Even more so, because his younger brother, Charles, also a priest of the Church of England, had experienced a similar feeling of 'strange warmth', which had led to his own conversion only three days earlier. As a result, a small group of Christians called the 'Holy Club' or the 'Bible Moths' became the founding fathers of the Methodist movement.

From that time on, and for more than forty years, John and Charles preached their new evangelistic understanding that it is not by good works, but by faith alone that we become Christians. Their movement grew rapidly. John travelled round the country, while Charles was based in London and in Bristol, where he preached in his New Room – which was constructed to cope with disapproving troublemakers. (The pulpit was completely inaccessible by the congregation.)

The first Methodists were persecuted and even satirised by society. The *London Magazine* of 1745 concluded that plans to complete a new bridge across the Thames had failed because the politicians had become Methodists, and now believed that bridge-building required faith rather than work.

Both brothers wrote poetry, and some of their poems have become well-known hymns. Charles produced nearly 9,000, although only a fraction are sung today.

'And can it be that I should gain' was published a year after Charles's conversion. It began as a poem called 'Free Grace', and the verses describe his own conversion experience. It opens with the poet's new understanding of the apostle Paul's letter to the Galatians:

Amazing love! How can it be
that thou, my God, shouldst die for me?

However, it is the lines in verse 4 that *Songs of Praise* viewers have mentioned time after time as they have voted for their favourite hymn:

My chains fell off, my heart was free,
I rose, went forth, and followed thee.

Charles had seen his own experience of being 'strangely warmed' as reminiscent of the story in Acts of Peter's release from prison.

Illustrating how well Charles's hymn has travelled through time to a very different world, one viewer remembers her own recovery from anorexia, with the help of Christian friends: '"My chains fell off, my heart was free," describes so clearly how I felt and continue to feel.'

And can it be that I should gain
  an interest in the Saviour's blood?
Died he for me, who caused his pain;
  for me, who him to death pursued?
Amazing love! How can it be
that thou, my God, shouldst die for me?

'Tis mystery all: the Immortal dies!
  Who can explore his strange design?
In vain the first-born seraph tries
  to sound the depths of love divine.
'Tis mercy all! Let earth adore,
let angel-minds enquire no more.

He left his Father's throne above –
  so free, so infinite his grace –
emptied himself of all but love,
  and bled for Adam's helpless race.
'Tis mercy all, immense and free;
for, O my God, it found out me!

Long my imprisoned spirit lay
  fast bound in sin and nature's night;
thine eye diffused a quickening ray –
  I woke, the dungeon flamed with light,
my chains fell off, my heart was free,
I rose, went forth, and followed thee.

No condemnation now I dread;
  Jesus, and all in him, is mine!
Alive in him, my living Head,
  and clothed in righteousness divine,
bold I approach the eternal throne,
and claim the crown, through Christ, my own.

And did those feet in ancient time
(JERUSALEM)

Words by William Blake (1757–1827)

Tune: C. Hubert H. Parry (1848–1918)

15

In a corner of St James's, Piccadilly, the London church close to the famous Piccadilly Circus, is an object of extraordinary beauty. It is a font carved in stone by the great artist Grinling Gibbons, who worked alongside Christopher Wren to rebuild London's churches after the great fire in 1666. Even on a dark winter's day, the font stands out. The slender shaft on which it rests has been sculpted to resemble the Tree of Life, and the bowl has been decorated in the most delicate relief with Adam and Eve, the ark and the baptism of Christ. It was here that the great poet William Blake was baptised in 1757.

Blake grew up in a London of striking contrasts. There were elegant new terraces, and areas of unimaginable squalor. The young artist was appalled by everyday street scenes, but from his window he could just see, through a narrow gap between dark, dismal warehouses, the Thames and the sylvan edge of the Surrey countryside. 'That is heaven,' he would say to friends, pointing out of the window.

Blake was described as a plain little man, with an astonishingly piercing way of looking at people. From childhood, what he claimed to see with those bright eyes included the face of God at his window and garden trees

'starred with angels'. For Blake, imagination was humankind's most holy possession, and the soul more real than the body. He wanted his painting and his poetry to make us search beyond the visible world, which he called 'the vegetable universe', to find universal truth.

'Jerusalem', the hymn well known to audiences around the world through the BBC's *Last Night of the Proms*, first appeared in a preface to a very long poem entitled 'Milton', in which Blake claimed to correct the errors of John Milton's *Paradise Lost*. The part of the poem sung as a hymn was written around 1804, when he was living at Felpham, on the coast of West Sussex. A regular *Songs of Praise* viewer wrote that they felt they could understand Blake's vision of the 'green and pleasant land' from their own happy experiences. But, as in all Blake's writing, there are many hidden layers of meaning behind every line. The 'vegetable universe', or rural Sussex, is only the starting point of a journey into the imagination.

The hymn takes up a legend that Joseph of Arimathea, a secret disciple of Jesus, came to England with the holy grail, the 'countenance divine', which

And did those feet in ancient time
  walk upon England's mountains green?
And was the holy Lamb of God
  on England's pleasant pastures seen?
And did the countenance divine
  shine forth upon our clouded hills?
And was Jerusalem builded here
  among those dark satanic mills?

Bring me my bow of burning gold!
  Bring me my arrows of desire!
Bring me my spear! O clouds, unfold!
  Bring me my chariot of fire!
I will not cease from mental fight,
  nor shall my sword sleep in my hand,
till we have built Jerusalem
  in England's green and pleasant land.

shone on the 'clouded hills', that is, the forceful new thinkers of eighteenth-century coffee houses and drawing rooms, who despised belief in the divine. Then there are the 'dark satanic mills'. At first sight, they appear to mean the great chimneys of the industrial revolution, belching fire and smoke like hell. Blake's real targets, however, were the new humanism, science and false religion emanating from the universities. He intended the very opposite of blind faith in calling for the 'bow of burning gold' (by which he meant human intelligence) to uncover ultimate truth so that all the peoples of earth would live for ever, safe in God's arms.

Blake would be astonished that 'Jerusalem', his tantalising poem, is sometimes described as a second national anthem. It has been bashed out on a million out-of-tune pianos to begin Women's Institute meetings; sung at countless music festivals; used to close suffragette meetings; and, of course, it is always belted out during the *Last Night of the Proms*. C. Hubert H. Parry's tune was intended to provide simple music to allow an audience to join in, and it did. The tune, which emerged during the darkest days of the First World War, liberated even the most reticent of English men and women to roar out, 'O clouds, unfold!' as a rallying cry to their cause. Oddly enough, for all its associations with Englishness, it first appeared in July 1915 in *Life and Work*, the Church of Scotland's magazine, where it ended with the words, 'In Scotland's fair and pleasant land'!

Be still, for the presence of the Lord

Words by David J. Evans (b. 1957)

Tune: 'Be Still' by David J. Evans

5

Be still,
for the presence of the Lord,
   the holy one, is here;
come bow before him now
   with reverence and fear:
      in him no sin is found –
      we stand on holy ground.
Be still,
for the presence of the Lord,
   the holy one, is here.

Be still,
for the glory of the Lord
   is shining all around;
he burns with holy fire,
   with splendour he is crowned:
      how awesome is the sight –
      our radiant King of light!
Be still,
for the glory of the Lord
   is shining all around.

Be still,
for the power of the Lord
   is moving in this place:
he comes to cleanse and heal,
   to minister his grace –
      no work too hard for him;
      in faith receive from him.
Be still,
for the power of the Lord
   is moving in this place.

We all have things that are sacred to us. For the *Songs of Praise* audience, a hymn can sometimes remind them of a crucial life experience, and can itself become part of their story – which they do not want to be spoiled, challenged or altered in any way. This is why it sometimes seems so important to them that the 'right' tune is broadcast for 'their' hymn.

Sometimes it can be the hymn itself that is sacred, especially for Christians who believe that it is 'anointed', written down through the inspiration of the Holy Spirit. Stories of hymns such as George Matheson's 'O love that wilt not let me go', or John Henry Newman's 'Praise to the Holiest in the height', being composed in a matter of minutes in some way seem to add to their mystique and significance. The hymn-writer Janet Wootton, reflecting on her own struggle for words, says Christians naturally long for some way of knowing that God is present in their songs, so the mystery of spontaneous inspiration has great appeal.

David Evans's song, 'Be still, for the presence of the Lord', is clearly inspired by words in the Bible, but seems to touch people where they are. Just singing it seems to give people a sense of God's presence, and it becomes a personal experience for them. Evans says that the core message of his hymn came from a phrase in the Old Testament: 'Then Jacob awoke from his sleep and said, "Surely the Lord is in this place and I did not know it."'

The sacredness of the Bible, expressed through the singing of psalms, can attract fierce passion as well as deep devotion. Johnston McKay, editor of religious broadcasting for BBC Scotland and producer of Radio 2's *Sunday Half-Hour* for many years, was astonished to be warned by a participant at a recording that the choir would 'rot in hell' – because a descant had been introduced for Psalm 23.

A Yorkshire newspaper report of 1820 describes how, at an evening service, a man in the congregation pulled out two loaded pistols and fired one at the organ gallery. As he was wrestled to the ground, he scattered pamphlets headed, '"The Abomination of Desolation" spoken of by Daniel the prophet that stands in the holy place is *the organ*. It is the image of the kingdom of Antichrist, the music.'

Although the report ends by saying, 'He was declared insane after examination at the police office in Leeds,' worship in which only unaccompanied singing of the psalms is permitted is still dear to some Christians. Producing an almost unearthly sound as they meditate line by line on the psalms, Gaelic-speaking members of the Free Church in Scotland's Outer Hebrides find their own sacred moments. They aim to strip away all distraction, in obedience to the Bible. Visiting film-makers often want to illustrate the strange sounds of their singing with stunning images of the landscape in which their plain stone churches sit – unaware that such visual pleasure is regarded by the singers themselves as one such distraction.

There are other less austere ways of experiencing the sacred and sensing God's presence, even at the most troubled times and in the most crowded places. 'Be still, for the presence of the Lord' created a sacred moment for presenter Pam Rhodes and other members of the *Songs of Praise* team. They were in St Paul's Cathedral, clearing away their equipment after the special programme broadcast live on the Sunday following the death of Diana, Princess of Wales. Somehow, a microphone had been left connected. The sound of an unknown young woman gently singing Evans's song helped the television team, together with thousands of others milling about sadly in the cathedral, to be still and remember that 'the power of the Lord is moving in this place'.

Be thou my vision, O Lord of my heart

Words: Irish (c. eighth century), translated by Mary Byrne (1880–1931) and Eleanor Hull (1860–1935)

Tune: 'Slane' (Irish traditional melody)

16

The beginning of every *Songs of Praise* recording is always a tense moment. Two days of rehearsal with the camera and sound crews and weeks of preparation by the BBC production team, and all the singers and musicians, at last come to a climax. Will millions of viewers be happy with the result? Producers know that people tend to switch channels if the first minute or so does not grab their attention.

For *Songs of Praise* for St Patrick's Day 2002, producer Maurice Maguire has cannily chosen a medley of popular hymns to begin a gala programme from Belfast. Superstars James Galway, Lesley Garrett and Daniel O'Donnell will be joining everyone in the packed Waterfront Hall, but it is the faces and voices of young and old singing 'Be thou my vision, O Lord of my heart' that are calculated to entice viewers to stay with the programme in the early stages.

'Now, let's hear from you singers right up at the back,' calls Paul Leddington Wright, one of *Songs of Praise*'s best-known conductors, waving telescopic arms up to the people in the gallery during the last minutes of rehearsal. 'Everyone else – listen!'

There follows a distant, hesitant sound. 'Stop! Stop!' shouts Paul to the singers far above his head, being shown in close-up on camera. 'Nice sound, but you all look miserable. Six million viewers need cheering up, and you can do it. Now.'

A bolder sound emerges in the next go, but Paul turns to the Methodist college choirs, sitting on stage with the Ulster Orchestra: 'Could you hear those angels in the gallery?'

'No-ooo!' chorus the college choirs, grinning broadly, determined to put their elders through their paces.

After the huge sound of the opening hymn, all eyes and ears are turned on the red-cassocked figure of BBC Radio 2's Choirboy of the Year, Nicholas Stenning, as he comes forward to sing solo the opening verse of 'Hail glorious St Patrick, dear saint of our isle'.

Later on in the evening, Nicholas is back. Betraying not the smallest sign of the nerves he felt during the long hours of rehearsal, he joins Lesley Garrett to sing a new setting of 'Ave Maria'. But before they can move onto the platform, there is a lot of backstage scurrying about, with much complicated technical setting up, supervised by director Medwyn Hughes from the mobile control van parked outside the hall. Stage managers speak confidently on their talkback to Hughes, so he will not be panicked by the fact that Garrett has gone missing. 'I can't go on,' protests her musical director, Philip Ellis. 'I do need a diva now.'

Be thou my vision, O Lord of my heart,
be all else but naught to me, save that thou art,
be thou my best thought in the day and the night,
both waking and sleeping, thy presence my light.

Be thou my wisdom, be thou my true word,
be thou ever with me, and I with thee, Lord,
be thou my great Father, and I thy true son,
be thou in me dwelling, and I with thee one.

Be thou my breastplate, my sword for the fight,
be thou my whole armour, be thou my true might,
be thou my soul's shelter, be thou my strong
    tower,
O raise thou me heavenward, great Power of my
    power.

Riches I heed not, nor man's empty praise,
be thou my inheritance now and always,
be thou and thou only the first in my heart,
O Sovereign of heaven, my treasure thou art.

High King of heaven, thou heaven's bright Sun,
O grant me its joys after vict'ry is won,
great heart of my own heart, whatever befall,
still be thou my vision, O Ruler of all.

When the diva at last appears, without fuss and radiating confidence, she and Nicholas are spotlit on the stage for a flawless performance. She tells Eamonn Holmes afterwards, 'As the singer, all I am is the conduit for something much greater than all of us.'

Two Irish women felt this same simple wish to be a conduit of grace, so gave the world the beautiful prayer hymn, 'Be thou my vision'. Mary Byrne translated the eighth-century Irish poem into English prose, and then her colleague, Eleanor Hull, turned the prose back into poetry. What emerged was one of the most personal of the nation's favourite hymns, whether sung to the tune 'Slane', or said in prayer.

As the congregation begins to sing 'Be thou my vision' in Belfast, *Songs of Praise* itself becomes the conduit for something greater. Series producer Michael Wakelin wants it to 'encourage people into an environment where they can make contact with their Maker and, at its best, be given a glimpse of the kingdom of God'.

Harpists at the St Patrick's Day 2002 broadcast from Belfast.

Brother, sister, let me serve you

Words by Richard Gillard (b. 1953)

Tune: 'Servant Song' by Richard Gillard

33

On Remembrance Sunday 2001, *Songs of Praise* came from York Minster. Viewers heard the stories of women at war – too often missing from the day when millions of casualties of war are remembered. Among the huge congregation, which included members of the Royal British Legion and all the armed services, were many brave women who had joined wartime organisations, such as the Women's Land Army. There were former ATS drivers, Wrens and women who had plotted the war fought in the air during the Battle of Britain in 1940.

Songs of Praise that day revealed plans for a new memorial to commemorate the unstinting service and sacrifice of so many women during the First and Second World Wars. The memorial will be placed near the Cenotaph in London, where every November women

German fighter planes over the English Channel during the Battle of Britain, which took place from July to October 1940.

join their male comrades to remember the fallen. Some of the stories were told by mothers. They recalled how, while gathering the harvest in the fields of Kent, they had looked up to see dogfights, then waves of bombers in the cloudless sky. 'Please, God, don't let it be too bad,' one remembered praying. 'Each one in the sky, friend or foe, was a mother's bairn.'

'Sometimes, we became aware that we were praying almost subconsciously,' said another woman, who was remembering fifty-two friends who had died in one air raid. 'We won't forget them.'

Although the programme focused on the stories of civilian women during wartime, viewers also met Lieutenant Colonel Jan Ransom. Filmed on the parade ground, Ransom, a career soldier, explained why the hymn 'Brother, sister, let me serve you' was the right one not only for her, but for all service personnel:

When I became a Christian, I wondered if there would be an opportunity to share my faith in the armed forces. I found myself in Northern Ireland soon after the Enniskillen bombing [of 1987], when so many people died. At first I found it very difficult being with soldiers who had been injured or lost friends. I hadn't suffered.

Then I realised I could say to them, 'I've been praying for you.' I had changed, no longer wanting to be in command by being powerful, but thinking more of the Bible and the verse: 'The Son of man came not to be served, but to serve.'

Appropriately, the motto of Sandhurst Military Academy, where Ransom trained as an officer, is 'Serve to Lead'.

The writer, Richard Gillard, describes how the song came into being:

It was in the first half of 1976 that I wrote verse 3 ('I will hold the Christ-light for you...'), but initially no more than that. It wasn't until one particularly summery Sunday afternoon in December 1976 or January 1977, back in Auckland, that I took that scrap of paper out of my guitar case and began to meditate on that single verse, exploring the possibilities that it suggested. I remember that the other four verses came quickly, though not in the order we now sing in the song.

Though it is hymn-like in form and sounded wonderful on the video tape of Songs of Praise, *played on York Minster's grand organ, I still prefer the down-to-earth groundedness of a guitar accompaniment and a simple folk-song treatment. But I let go of it long ago and have very little to say any more. And that's as it should be.*

Brother, sister, let me serve you,
  let me be as Christ to you;
pray that I may have the grace to
  let you be my servant too.

We are pilgrims on a journey,
  and companions on the road;
we are here to help each other
  walk the mile and bear the load.

I will hold the Christ-light for you
  in the night-time of your fear;
I will hold my hand out to you,
  speak the peace you long to hear.

I will weep when you are weeping;
  when you laugh I'll laugh with you;
I will share your joy and sorrow
  till we've seen this journey through.

When we sing to God in heaven
  we shall find such harmony,
born of all we've known together
  of Christ's love and agony.

Brother, sister, let me serve you,
  let me be as Christ to you;
pray that I may have the grace to
  let you be my servant too.

Come down, O Love Divine

Words by Bianco da Siena (d. 1434), translated by Richard Frederick Littledale (1833–90)

Tune: 'Down Ampney' by Ralph Vaughan Williams (1872–1958)

40

Not far from the source of the River Thames on the edge of the Cotswolds is the village of Down Ampney, where the composer Ralph Vaughan Williams was born. His great uncle was Charles Darwin, so his religious upbringing was not entirely orthodox. Answering her young son's questions, Vaughan Williams's mother said, 'The Bible says that God made the world in six days; great uncle Charles thinks it took longer, but we need not worry, for it is equally wonderful either way.'

The Church of All Saints, Down Ampney, Gloucestershire.

Vaughan Williams's involvement with church music began when he served briefly as an organist in Lambeth. He gave up because he felt that Church of England worship did no justice either to music or to faith, so it is surprising that the young composer, who described himself as 'a cheerful agnostic', was then appointed musical editor of the *English Hymnal*. Although the Church of England had never had an official hymn book, *Hymns Ancient and Modern*, in common use since the 1860s, enshrined for many the doctrine of the church.

First published in 1906, the *English Hymnal* created something of a hymn-book revolution. Its editor reintroduced the music of the pre-Reformation church as well as using music handed down over generations of English families. In 1903, Vaughan Williams began to note down some of the old folk tunes that were still to be heard in the countryside. When he collected his first song in Essex, Mr Pottipher, the singer, told him, 'If you can get the words, the Lord sends you a tune!'

'Every village was a nest of singing birds,' said Cecil Sharp, who in the 1880s revived interest in the English folk-song tradition.

In the late 1960s, before starting to produce *Songs of Praise*, I worked as a sound recordist on a film about Vaughan Williams. With the composer's widow, Ursula, we met Maud Karpeles, who had collected songs with Vaughan Williams. One woman they visited at Monks Gate in Sussex sang them a song called 'Our Captain Calls'. The tune had found a new lease of life in the *English Hymnal* as an accompaniment to John

Come down, O Love Divine,
  seek thou this soul of mine,
and visit it with thine own ardour glowing;
  O Comforter, draw near,
  within my heart appear,
and kindle it, thy holy flame bestowing.

O let it freely burn,
  till earthly passions turn
to dust and ashes in its heat consuming;
  and let thy glorious light
  shine ever on my sight,
and clothe me round, the while my path illuming.

Let holy charity
  mine outward vesture be,
and lowliness become mine inner clothing;
  true lowliness of heart,
  which takes the humbler part,
and o'er its own shortcomings weeps with loathing.

And so the yearning strong
  with which the soul will long,
shall far outpass the power of human telling;
  for none can guess its grace,
  till he become the place
wherein the Holy Spirit makes his dwelling.

Bunyan's words, 'He who would valiant be'.

As musical editor of the *English Hymnal*, Vaughan Williams took a very firm line. The duty of a collector of folk songs was to give them back to the world, so the tunes used in the new hymn book were to be pitched low enough to allow everyone in the congregation a chance to sing. Hymns were the folk music of the church, so it was time to exclude Victorian tunes that were enervating or sentimental. What was needed were tunes that were beautiful and noble.

The new hymn book also reintroduced plainchant and hymns from the daily offices, or services, of the pre-Reformation service books. But the launch of the *English Hymnal* was very unpromising. Randall Davidson, the then Archbishop of Canterbury, said he hoped his clergy would not use it at all.

The Bishop of Bristol went further, and banned it on the grounds that 'some of the Saint's Day hymns are contrary to the teaching of the Church of England'.

But others gave it a cautious welcome, and the vicar of St Peter's, Cranley Gardens, in London wrote of the Bristol ban in his November 1906 parish letter: 'It is very doubtful whether the Bishop of Bristol is right in his contention.' But even he seems to have sat on the fence somewhat, as he went on to appeal for a 'disused' violin and more copies of *Hymns Ancient and Modern*. He also sought a 'volunteer' to review the new hymn book for him: 'One must be a folk-lore enthusiast not to resent having a traditional melody forced upon one at every turn, instead of something just as "English" but well known,' complained the anonymous reviewer.

Nethertheless, Vaughan Williams had begun a revolution in hymn-singing. He composed four new tunes for the *English Hymnal*, all of which are still regularly included in *Songs of Praise*. The tune 'Down Ampney', named after his birthplace in the Gloucestershire countryside, is said to be the most beautiful of all. Vaughan Williams wrote the tune for a translation of some fifteenth-century Italian verse, '*Discendi, amor santo*': 'Come down, O Love Divine'.

Dear Lord and Father of mankind

Words by John Greenleaf Whittier (1807–92)
Tune: 'Repton' by C. Hubert H. Parry (1848–1918)

2

How is our second-most-popular hymn connected to a mind-blowing drug? And how did a nineteenth-century Quaker become known as the greatest American hymn-writer?

In Haverhill, Massachusetts, part of the gentle North American landscape of New England where some of the first European settlers lived, there stands a big white clapboard farmhouse built by the Society of Friends, or the Quakers, in 1688. John Greenleaf Whittier was born in this house in 1807, when Haverhill was still an entirely Quaker community. He grew up with neighbours for whom worship meant gathering in the meeting house and waiting in prayerful silence for the Holy Spirit to move them to speak.

Young Whittier wanted to be a poet, but his father resisted him, saying that 'poetry would not give him bread'. He became a journalist instead, but when his father died, he had to return home to run the family farm. He soon found that he could not cope with the physical labour of farming.

At this time, slavery was a burning issue in the United States. Using his journalistic skills, Whittier took up the anti-slavery cause, calling it 'the national crime'. He was frequently abused and attacked, but he was not afraid of unpopularity, and he found great solace in writing poetry.

In 1872, he wrote what he called a 'hymn-poem': 'The Brewing of Soma'. It had seventeen verses, and verse 12 is the start of the hymn that *Songs of Praise* viewers have voted into second place: 'Dear Lord and Father of mankind'.

And the first eleven verses? The clue lies in the title of the original poem. The 'soma' that Whittier described in the poem was a drug – a potent drink brewed by Hindu priests that induced wild and uncontrollable behaviour.

'Dear Lord and Father of mankind' is often chosen as a wedding hymn. However, John Bell, himself a hymn-writer and compiler, says it is really a penitential hymn and a peculiar choice for a wedding service. The line 'forgive our foolish ways' sung at a marriage union seems very odd to him, and the words, 'breathe through the heats of our desire' also sound strangely out of place at such a 'passionate moment'. And yet it remains a perennial favourite.

The hymn evokes memories other than of weddings for many *Songs of Praise* viewers. The line 'O Sabbath rest by Galilee' reminds them of Holy Land pilgrimages, during which they have sung the hymn standing at the water's edge. Choirs drawn from the audience of Radio 4's *Daily Service* have even broadcast the hymn live from the shores of Lake Galilee in modern Israel Palestine.

John Bell believes that Hubert Parry's gentle, pastoral tune 'Repton' accounts for the hymn's enormous popularity as much as the words. It is a 'soft' tune that creates a feeling of well-being. Even in the most worrying times, it can help us forget our cares. Even if you cannot remember the words, just humming or whistling the tune can be beneficial.

The experience of the power of a whistled hymn tune is mentioned in *Why We Shall Win*, a 1914 edition of a weekly paper, *London Opinion*, which described life in the capital in the first weeks of the First World War. The writer watches a long column of grenadier guards coming to the end of a long route march near Hyde Park Corner, singing as they pass:

The air that brought tears into my eyes and shook me to the soul was not a song at all. It was a hymn tune. The guards whistled it as they marched. Believe me, the poignancy of the tune was heartbreaking. It was so indubitably British, and these were British lads in the splendour of their manhood, going ere long to die if need be for everything we reverence...

The songs pass on, but the old hymn tunes remain in the memory... the cajoleries of the Kaiser cannot break a brotherhood based upon the Bible, our hymn tunes and the English language.

Nearly ninety years later, as choirs in the Royal Albert Hall celebrated another New Year with *Songs of Praise*, the words 'Drop thy still dews of quietness', sung unaccompanied and with great fervour, seemed to show that an American Quaker's hymn sung to a Welshman's tune still has the power to help us as we try to find that 'still small voice of calm'.

Dear Lord and Father of mankind,
  forgive our foolish ways!
Reclothe us in our rightful mind;
in purer lives thy service find,
  in deeper reverence, praise.

In simple trust like theirs who heard
  beside the Syrian sea
the gracious calling of the Lord,
let us, like them, without a word,
  rise up and follow thee.

O Sabbath rest by Galilee!
  O calm of hills above,
where Jesus knelt to share with thee
the silence of eternity
  interpreted by love!

With that deep hush subduing all
  our words and works that drown
the tender whisper of thy call,
as noiseless let thy blessing fall
  as fell thy manna down.

Drop thy still dews of quietness,
  till all our strivings cease;
take from our souls the strain and stress,
and let our ordered lives confess
  the beauty of thy peace.

Breathe through the heats of our desire
  thy coolness and thy balm;
let sense be dumb, let flesh retire;
speak through the earthquake, wind, and fire,
  O still small voice of calm!

Eternal Father, strong to save

Words by William Whiting (1825–78)

Tune: 'Melita' by John Bacchus Dykes (1823–76)

35

In the middle of the night, audible above the shrieking wind and the rain spattering on the windows, comes the crack of two maroons. Most people living in the little seaside town turn over and go back to sleep. Only a handful of hardy volunteers will be racing down to the harbour to do a job few of us would be brave enough to do. The insomniac up the hill overlooking the quay glimpses the flashing lights of the lifeboat as it roars out into the sea at its wildest.

> Eternal Father, strong to save,
> whose arm doth bind the restless wave,
> who bidd'st the mighty ocean deep
> its own appointed limits keep;
>   O hear us when we cry to thee
>   for those in peril on the sea.
>
> O Saviour, whose almighty word
> the winds and waves submissive heard,
> who walkedst on the foaming deep,
> and calm amid its rage didst sleep:
>   O hear us when we cry to thee
>   for those in peril on the sea.
>
> O sacred Spirit, who didst brood
> upon the chaos dark and rude,
> who bad'st its angry tumult cease,
> and gavest light and life and peace:
>   O hear us when we cry to thee
>   for those in peril on the sea.
>
> O Trinity of love and power,
> our brethren shield in danger's hour;
> from rock and tempest, fire and foe,
> protect them wheresoe'er they go:
>   and ever let there rise to thee
>   glad hymns of praise from land and sea.

Lives are in danger, and we must pray 'for those in peril on the sea'.

Such is the life of the many volunteer crews of the Royal National Lifeboat Institution, who are on call day and night. Their story has been told time and time again on *Songs of Praise*. It was first featured in a programme made in the mid-1970s directed by Ray Short, who arranged a huge choir around the Walmer Lifeboat, which was pulled up onto the pebbled beach beside the calmest of seas. The pictures and stories from that evening gave birth to the idea of filming people at work and at home, and them choosing their favourite hymns. When the new-style *Songs of Praise*, with interviews, started in 1977, lifeboats were soon sent careering into the sea all around Britain as coxswains, mechanics and ever-faithful secretaries chose 'Eternal Father, strong to save'.

For me, it is a hymn that brings many images to mind. Presenters and film crews for *Songs of Praise* have often found themselves plunging through huge waves in inshore rescue boats, and Diane-Louise Jordan was even the guinea pig in a dramatic reconstruction of an air-sea rescue. William Whiting's famous words have been amended and added to (as in the 2002 edition of *Songs of Praise* from Lossiemouth in Scotland), to remember the search-and-rescue aircrews who nowadays join the lifeboat men in risking their lives on our behalf:

Lord of the heavens, by whose might
   mankind has learned the skill of flight,
to span the world from land to land
   released from earth's restraining hand.
Be with us, Father, as we rise
   to brave the challenge of the skies.

Another picture is of a 1978 edition of *Songs of Praise*, which was filmed and recorded at the famous (but now closed) Chatham Naval Base. Among the congregation was the team that serviced and supplied

HMS *Endeavour* for her then-regular peacetime tours to the Falkland Islands. The programme ended with 'Sunset', played by the Royal Marines Band, followed by the last verse of 'Eternal Father, strong to save', sung as a prayer. Little did Captain Anthony Tippet know then that, in May 1982, as vice-admiral and chief of fleet support, he would have the daunting responsibility of making the naval task force ready, in just a few days, to sail for war in the South Atlantic.

Every year a church choir moves through London's Royal Albert Hall, along with men and women from all the services, shortly before the climax of the annual Royal British Legion Festival of Remembrance. It is not only during the moment when red poppies float in their thousands onto young sailor and old soldier alike that we remember the sacrifice of lives lost in conflict. In November 2002, fading news film from twenty years ago of the attack on HMS *Sheffield* during the Falklands War comes vividly to mind as the Royal Albert Hall resounds once more to John Bacchus Dykes's great tune, 'Melita'.

'Melita' means Malta, and this evokes yet another image. Tourists visit the island of Malta, which fought so bravely during the Second World War, in high summer. These are the long hot days when the island is sun-baked, and holidaymakers in the traditional white houses around the rocky shores of St Paul's bay look out on a calm, blue sea. However, we are misled by this tranquil scene; St Paul's bay is aptly named, for it was here that the apostle Paul was shipwrecked in a violent storm almost 2,000 years ago.

William Whiting wrote 'Eternal Father, strong to save' in 1860. It appeared in the very first edition of *Hymns Ancient and Modern* in 1861, having been commissioned by Henry Baker, the son of another vice-admiral. Baker was the prime mover in compiling *Hymns Ancient and Modern*, and he was said to have had an uncanny knack for spotting winners. Although he lived far from the sea, in deepest Herefordshire, his father's experiences in Queen Victoria's Navy must have made as deep an impression on him as the hymn still makes on us today.

From heaven you came, helpless babe
(THE SERVANT KING)

Words by Graham Kendrick (b. 1950)

Tune: 'The Servant King' by Graham Kendrick

Hidden away in a worship song I thought I knew, having included it so often in the religious programmes that I have produced, is a line that many *Songs of Praise* viewers have pointed to as the reason why 'The Servant King' is in their top forty. Now I have heard the song again, I cannot understand how I missed it.

Look, says the singer, come and see 'hands that flung stars into space to cruel nails surrendered'. It demonstrates the skill of the hymn-writer, for here in two lines of poetry is an image that I risk taking several pages trying to describe in my own words.

From heaven you came, helpless babe,
entered our world, your glory veiled;
not to be served but to serve,
and give your life that we might live.

This is our God, the Servant King,
he calls us now to follow him,
to bring our lives as a daily offering
of worship to the Servant King.

There in the garden of tears,
my heavy load he chose to bear;
his heart with sorrow was torn,
'Yet not my will but yours,' he said.

Come see his hands and his feet,
the scars that speak of sacrifice,
hands that flung stars into space
to cruel nails surrendered.

So let us learn how to serve,
and in our lives enthrone him;
each other's needs to prefer,
for it is Christ we're serving.

Graham Kendrick's most-quoted lines are in the third verse of this song of devotion, which begins by directly addressing the God of creation, who is also the child of Bethlehem and the man who gave his life 'that we might live'.

John Bell is a hymn-writer from a different church

UN soldiers help villagers to rebuild their homes in Maklenovac, Bosnia.

tradition, but he has shared the Greenbelt experience with Kendrick, and has great respect for his songs: 'There are hard words which God may have to say to us, which we don't want to hear. Kendrick is one of too few writers in the Western world today who allows the sadness at the dark side in our lives to be articulated in a song.'

Bell points out that John Calvin, Martin Luther and all the great reformers expected that everyone would worship privately before they came together in public worship: 'They heard the majestic and prophetic word in the light of their private prayers at home.' He thinks 'The Servant King' is a song to be sung quietly and reflectively, and not triumphantly. 'Hands that flung stars into space' is a line to ponder, and Bell wishes that overhead-projector or power-point presentation of the words was not increasingly popular.

Perhaps that is why, as a TV director, these words, noticed by the audience, had passed me by. When I was series producer of *Songs of Praise* I was not in favour of putting the words on the TV screen. Until quite recently, *Radio Times* carried the list of hymns to be sung in the programme, and some viewers would look them up in their own books. Many listeners had the *BBC Hymn Book*, published after the Second World War, which helped them to take part in Radio 4's *Daily Service*. Alas, it was hardly used at all in churches, but today the new *BBC Songs of Praise* hymn book, published in 1997, allows viewers to look up the hymns they enjoy, and this has found its way into some churches.

As Bell says, 'You don't want something that takes words like this away as soon as you've sung them. You need the book, the eye and the intellect, as well as the emotions. Like all the best poetry, it takes the second or third reading before the impact comes.'

'The Servant King' was written in 1984 for Greenbelt, a big open-air festival of Christian arts, with younger Christians in mind. Kendrick has described how he first picked out the tune on a piano at home. He says his children, who in those days had to be coaxed to sleep before their father could work at his composing, would not sing his songs today. Fortunately, according to *Songs of Praise* audiences both young and old, they are in the minority.

Great is thy faithfulness, O God my Father

Words by Thomas O. Chisholm (1866–1960)

Tune: 'Faithfulness' by William Runyan (1870–1957)

4

'I was thoroughly gazumped by him and his hymn!' laughs Ruth Pashley, indicating her husband Trevor as she remembers her interview 'that nearly was' for *Songs of Praise*, and the filming they say changed their lives.

In 1993, a BBC team descended on the Pashleys' home in South Yorkshire to film them both for a programme being recorded in the Meadowhall shopping centre. They were originally chosen because Ruth, a former social worker, had vivid memories of Billy Graham's early crusades, while Trevor had sung in the Sheffield celebration choir formed for Graham's 1984 campaign.

The BBC had not known that both Ruth and Trevor were coping with great difficulties in their lives. Trevor has suffered from Parkinson's disease for many years; the first symptoms appeared not long after his nightly contribution to the celebration choir that heralded Billy Graham. Ruth has bone and muscle problems, and chronic arthritis, and she is permanently in pain. Researcher Sue and director Diane Reid listened to the Pashleys' striking story of faith and endurance. At such a point, the journalist, even a religious programme researcher, wonders whether such affliction turns the sufferer against God. In this case, however, Ruth and Trevor's response provided the inspirational ingredient that infuses so many *Songs of Praise* programmes.

Trevor, after an energetic working life in the now-closed Parkgate Steelworks, and as a diesel-engine mechanic for the coal board, can only move with great difficulty. Yet he still manages to drive, and, with Ruth, he is running a helpline for fellow sufferers. He convinced Diane Reid and producer John Forrest, who admitted they had never been to a football match, that they were missing a great experience. Trevor is in the stand at Bramhall Lane most Saturdays in the season, supporting Sheffield United. 'Not doing too well,' he reported to me, early in 2002, adding with wicked

> Great is thy faithfulness, O God my Father,
>   there is no shadow of turning with thee;
> thou changest not, thy compassions, they fail not;
>   as thou hast been thou for ever wilt be.
>
> *Great is thy faithfulness, great is thy faithfulness,*
>   *morning by morning new mercies I see;*
> *all I have needed thy hand hath provided,*
>   *great is thy faithfulness, Lord, unto me.*
>
> Summer and winter, and springtime and harvest,
>   sun, moon and stars in their courses above,
> join with all nature in manifold witness
>   to thy great faithfulness, mercy and love.
>
> Pardon for sin and a peace that endureth,
>   thine own dear presence to cheer and to guide;
> strength for today and bright hope for tomorrow,
>   blessings all mine, with ten thousand beside!

pleasure, 'but better than Sheffield Wednesday.' He told presenter Pam Rhodes on camera:

It's true that I was on the mountain top one minute, and in the valley the next. But we thought, after we'd heard the doctor's diagnosis, we can't let this thing get topsides of us. So we've always had a positive attitude.

We've had to work hard to not let it get us down, and I do sometimes wake up feeling really depressed. But then I make myself get up to stop thinking about myself. You can always write down some of God's blessings. I look at my home and garden – well, it's not a stately home, but it's nice – my lovely wife and my kids and grandchildren, and the balance sheet of life is good, isn't it?

When it started, I thought I was redundant. But if my shaking gets people's attention, then I can tell them how good I think God's been to me, and then I'm working for God.

Yes, people do say, 'You've been a religious person, why should you end up like this?' But without it, I wouldn't have had so many doors opened to me.

They were both filmed, but there is not much evidence of Ruth. Sitting in their small, comfortable living room, Ruth and Trevor look back at their 'bit' in *Songs of Praise*. Ruth points out the lovely close-up of her grandson Jack, then a baby. 'The BBC wanted him in; he really caught their eye,' she says, 'but he got a bit tired, so for most of the filming I was upstairs keeping him quiet and happy. If you're quick, you will just catch a glimpse of me!'

'God's shown great faithfulness to me,' says Trevor on the film, which is why Diane Reid suggested Thomas O. Chisholm's gospel song, made so famous by Billy Graham at his 1954 Harringay Crusade, to illustrate Trevor's experience. Diane also asked Trevor to write and say the final prayer for that edition of *Songs of Praise*:

Heavenly Father,
we praise you for the gift of music,
for the ability to express it
and the opportunity to share it.
May our efforts this evening
bring praise, honour and glory
to your Name. Amen.

Guide me, O thou great Redeemer

Words by William Williams (1717–91), Peter Williams (1727–96) and others

Tune: 'Cwm Rhondda' by John Hughes (1873–1932)

11

On an autumn morning in 2001, a sad congregation in Westminster Abbey suddenly began to feel a little better as the great tune 'Cwm Rhondda' sounded triumphantly from the organ. Led by the men of the London Welsh Male Voice Choir, resplendent in their red jackets, and in the presence of his royal highness, the Prince of Wales, everyone rose to their feet and roared out 'Guide me, O thou great Redeemer'. William Williams's best-known hymn was just the right way to remember Harry Secombe, who so loved this great hymn from his homeland. For me, it brought back the memory of his impromptu rendering of 'Cwm Rhondda' in a run-down London street, which drew a crowd of shoppers, largely exiles from Cardiff's Tiger Bay, who fell joyfully on their fellow countryman. 'You've made our street come good,' they called out to Harry.

It was another singer – known as 'the sweet singer of Wales' – who wrote the hymn in 1745. He was extraordinarily prolific, writing more than 1,000 other hymns, mostly in the Welsh language. Although he translated the first verse into English, we owe it to a completely unrelated Peter Williams for the translation of the other verses. Very few of his other 1,000 hymns have ever been translated.

William Williams grew up in Pantycelyn, rural Wales. When he was twenty he went out of curiosity to hear a fiery Calvinist preacher, Howell Harris, who was himself only twenty-one. The experience set the young Williams on the road he so powerfully depicts in the hymn. As a travelling preacher, his oratory played a huge part in the eighteenth-century evangelical revival in Wales.

Mine workings and miners' cottages in the Rhondda Valley, 1952.

Guide me, O thou great Redeemer,
  pilgrim through this barren land;
I am weak, but thou art mighty,
  hold me with thy powerful hand:
    bread of heaven,
feed me till I want no more.

Open now the crystal fountain
  whence the healing stream doth flow;
let the fire and cloudy pillar
  lead me all my journey through:
    strong deliverer,
be thou still my strength and shield.

When I tread the verge of Jordan,
  bid my anxious fears subside;
death of death, and hell's destruction,
  land me safe on Canaan's side:
    songs of praises
I will ever give to thee.

Many of Williams's hymns were probably originally written to be read as poetry within his sermons, and the fervour of their language captivated the crowd. Williams could truthfully describe all Wales as his 'parish', as for more than forty years he travelled almost 100,000 miles, preaching mostly in the open air. On several occasions, he was set on by a mob, most likely hired by local gentry, who thought the original words, 'Guide me, O thou great Jehovah' – which drew on the Old Testament story of the Israelites' journey to the Promised Land – and references to 'death of death and hell's destruction' threatened the feudal order.

Even so, what would be the impact of this hymn without the magnificent tune 'Cwm Rhondda'? John Hughes wrote it for a choir festival in 1905, 150 years after Williams wrote the words. Hughes worked on the old Great Western Railway, but was also a precentor at his local church in Pontypridd.

In a TV film of 1967, miners and their wives remembered the hard days of coal and chapel in the Rhondda, the narrow valley where terrace houses still line the narrow streets. Old men described how they would sing 'Cwm Rhondda' going down in the cage to the coalface: 'It was the Welsh way of life.' Every boy in every family had gone to work at the age of twelve, earning less than ten old pence a day. 'When I got a shilling's pocket money back from my mother,' said one, 'I thought I was the lord mayor of this locality!'

Another said that 'Young men were in the cemetery before their time, but the womenfolk had an even harder time than their husbands,' trying to feed and clothe a growing family on such tiny wages. The hope of the Promised Land was to be found in politics as well as in religion. During the coal strike of the 1920s, the chapel, where their obedience to the mine as well as to God was monitored by colliery managers, took on a new role as a soup kitchen, which was set up in the vestry for the children.

Today, the mines are all closed and the valley is green again. The pitgear of one mine is preserved as a heritage site, and visitors there catch the distant, unearthly sound from a tape quietly but endlessly playing 'Cwm Rhondda'. The choruses of 'Cwm Rhondda' sung by Welsh rugby supporters echo faintly but firmly the biblical inspiration of William Williams, 'the sweet singer of Wales'.

I, the Lord of sea and sky

(HERE I AM, LORD)

Words by Daniel L. Schutte (b. 1947)

Tune: 'Here I Am, Lord' by Daniel L. Schutte

17

I, the Lord of sea and sky,
I have heard my people cry.
All who dwell in dark and sin
my hand will save.
I, who made the stars of night,
I will make their darkness bright.
Who will bear my light to them?
Whom shall I send?

Here I am, Lord. Is it I, Lord?
I have heard you calling in the night.
I will go, Lord, if you lead me.
I will hold your people in my heart.

I, the Lord of snow and rain,
I have borne my people's pain.
I have wept for love of them.
They turn away.
I will break their hearts of stone,
give them hearts for love alone.
I will speak my word to them.
Whom shall I send?

I, the Lord of wind and flame,
I will tend the poor and lame.
I will set a feast for them.
My hand will save.
Finest bread I will provide
till their hearts be satisfied.
I will give my life to them.
Whom shall I send?

Out of towering clouds, the RAF helicopter emerges into clear, blue sky far above the dark waters of the North Sea. The aircraft is a small human capsule dwarfed by the immensity of creation as it returns successfully from another rescue mission. Perhaps a seaman has been plucked from the sea, or an injured mountaineer recovered from a snowfield and brought to safety by caring hands and through efficient teamwork.

For the Christian fisherman in danger out at sea, the mountaineer or the pilot in the sky, these are the times when they are most aware of the 'Lord of sea and sky' to whom Daniel Schutte gives voice in this increasingly requested worship song. When Diane-Louise Jordan introduced a recent programme from RAF Lossiemouth, on the northeast coast of Scotland, we saw her being winched up from the waves to the safety of the helicopter. It was a dramatic prelude to the hymn; Corporal Matthew Little sang the opening verse as a solo, and the congregation in the base chapel then joined in with the chorus, 'Here I am, Lord'. This time, the rescue was only a practice exercise, but sometimes it is a matter of life and death.

Many *Songs of Praise* viewers write to the programme about why they value this particular song. 'It means a lot when you are in a crisis,' wrote one.

For another, 'It helped us make a decision when we wanted to start a new Christian community, and wondered if we could cope.'

'It's brill to use as a reflection,' wrote one young viewer.

Gordon Stewart, a *Songs of Praise* conductor, says the hymn always reminds him of the moving moment when his friend was consecrated as a bishop, and the huge burden that he was accepting.

Quite unusually for a popular-hymn-writer, Schutte is a Roman Catholic. Much of his inspiration comes from years of parish work as a musical director. 'For me, the important thing is that the music connects with people's souls,' writes Schutte, who is composer-in-residence at the University of San Francisco. 'It's meant to lead people to prayer and for people to participate in.'

After long experience as an organist in an Anglican cathedral, it has been a revelation for musician and composer David Thorne to become director of music in Portsmouth's Roman Catholic Cathedral. 'It is amazing to me how, musically, the Catholic Church has embraced the evangelical style.'

Portsmouth's Catholic cathedral, with its fine acoustic, has a strong musical tradition, and Sunday Masses are sung in both new and old styles to suit a large and diverse community. A cantor leads at some Masses, but Thorne finds that, given a lead from the organ, everyone is prepared to join in the singing. 'I use a full organ accompaniment; I find the more you give, the more people sing.' The 100th anniversary of the cathedral was marked with the restoration of their fine three-manual organ, and Radio 2's *Sunday Half-Hour* celebrated the Queen's golden jubilee with a special programme from there.

Thorne is no stranger to innovation. While working for ITV in the 1980s, I devised a programme called *Dial a Hymn*, which was intended to challenge *Songs of Praise*. It had the simple format of responding 'live' to viewers telephoning from home with their requests, and arranging for their chosen hymns to be sung for them. One of the most successful editions of *Dial a Hymn* came from Portsmouth's Anglican cathedral. It was presented by Fern Britton, and Thorne, as conductor, successfully overcame his feelings of terror as the complete spectrum of hymn tunes was tossed at him by callers. It was a rough and ready format, but Thorne and the present Bishop of Salisbury, David Stancliffe, who shared in conversations with viewers that night, both remember how they and a large congregation discovered how to be the 'servant church' on TV. If Schutte's song had been as popular then as it is now, it would have been as perfect a choice for *Dial a Hymn* from Portsmouth as it was more recently on *Songs of Praise*'s visit to the air-sea rescue team.

In heavenly love abiding

Words by Anna L. Waring (1823–1910)

Tune: 'Penlan' by David Jenkins (1848–1915)

24

Anna Waring began life as a Quaker, and later became an Anglican. Born in South Wales, she devoted much of her life to prison visiting and looking after ex-prisoners. Anna wanted to write something for them, and for all people who felt cut off from church life, people who were, for whatever reason, outside the church. Her hymn, 'In heavenly love abiding', must have helped many a convict in the grim Victorian jails, with its reassurance of God's ever-present help in trouble, and its confidence of better times to come. The hymn is based on Psalm 23, and 'my treasure' in the last verse means the singer's heart. And perhaps that is why it is still loved and chosen so often by the housebound audience of *Songs of Praise*. Religious broadcasts always receive many letters from listeners and viewers looking for comfort and support.

It seems that 'In heavenly love abiding' was first broadcast as long ago as 1885. On 4 November of that year, telephone subscribers in the north of England were 'amazed and comforted' upon hearing it through their receivers, as the congregation of St Paul's, Manningham, in Bradford, sang it to the emotional tune 'Penlan'. When BBC broadcasts began properly in 1922, it was not long before listeners to 6BM, the Bournemouth station, were offered a monthly service of hymns and a religious address especially for the sick. Later in the 1920s, Kathleen Cordeaux, a listener to

2LO, the London station, began a campaign to persuade John Reith, the first director general of the BBC, to broadcast a daily evensong for the sick. What followed was described as the 'happiest of new ventures': a daily radio service of hymns and prayers, broadcast each morning to the whole of Britain from the heart of the BBC at Savoy Hill in London.

Dick Sheppard of St Martin-in-the-Fields, the first 'radio preacher', said of the service in the 1929 *BBC Handbook*, 'I am sometimes a little impatient at the idea that it is a boon to invalids only, for I know many who love to have those few minutes of carefully directed daily prayer, some of them even while they carry on with household tasks.' Some listeners went further and arranged for the radio to be heard in the servants' hall so that staff would stop work and join in the hymns. In 1932, the *Daily Service* was broadcast from its own 'religious' studio in the new Broadcasting House in London, but the studio was destroyed by a bomb during the Second World War.

Sunday Half-Hour was born because of a wartime need for the BBC to provide programmes for the British Expeditionary Force in France in 1940. Although it does not have quite as formidably long a record as the *Daily Service*, *Sunday Half-Hour* is itself over sixty years old and still going strong. A huge audience of all ages still keeps its Sunday-evening date with today's popular presenter, Roger Royle, and 'In heavenly love abiding' is

In heavenly love abiding,
   no change my heart shall fear;
and safe is such confiding,
   for nothing changes here.
The storm may roar without me,
   my heart may low be laid,
but God is round about me,
   and can I be dismayed?

Wherever he may guide me,
   no want shall turn me back;
my shepherd is beside me,
   and nothing can I lack.
His wisdom ever waketh,
   his sight is never dim,
he knows the way he taketh,
   and I will walk with him.

Green pastures are before me,
   which yet I have not seen;
bright skies will soon be o'er me,
   where the dark clouds have been.
My hope I cannot measure,
   my path to life is free,
my Saviour has my treasure
   and he will walk with me.

still often requested. With its sound of hymns being sung in every part of the world, *Sunday Half-Hour* has survived unscathed, despite the original *Forces Programme Network* becoming the *Light Programme* and then Radio 2. It would be fascinating to know if there are still survivors from among those who sang under the direction of conductor Walford Davies during the first live broadcast of the programme, from St Mary Redcliffe Church, Bristol. It was a thundery night in 1940, and the first hymn sung in the vast nave was 'We love the place, O God'. Later that night, the church survived a bombing raid on the city.

The tune for 'In heavenly love abiding', 'Penlan', was written by a Welshman, David Jenkins, a professor of music and church precentor. Many conductors and religious producers understand the dangers inherent in an emotional tune that sometimes encourages the singer to go over the top. It was once described unkindly at the Church of Scotland's General Assembly: 'The tenor part', said one elder, 'has been subjected to the introduction of a great number of quavers and semiquavers, running up and down the scale like rabbits on a Welsh mountain.'

'No matter,' says today's *Songs of Praise* series producer, Michael Wakelin. 'I love it to death!'

Just as I am, without one plea

Words by Charlotte Elliott (1789–1871)

Tunes: 'Saffron Walden' by A.H. Brown (1830–1926); 'Wordsworth' by William Bradbury (1816–68)

The story of the writing of this hymn has all the ingredients of a Victorian melodrama. Charlotte Elliott was an invalid all her life. After growing up in her father's vicarage in Clapham, she went to live with her brother, also a clergyman, in Brighton. One day, in 1834, he was holding a bazaar to raise money to help start a school for the daughters of poor clergy, and wanted his sister to help him run it. But Charlotte felt too ill that day, and she lay in bed feeling utterly useless. There seemed to be nothing she could offer.

Then, as the story goes, she remembered something an evangelist visiting her father's parish had once said to her, years before. She had been defending her lack of interest in Christianity by arguing that Jesus was for the pious and the exceptionally good, certainly not for the weak

and sickly. 'Come to him, just as you are,' the evangelist had replied.

The phrase 'just as I am' came to her mind that day in Brighton, as she lay in despair, and she began to write out a statement of the Christian faith that she had known for so long, but had never before felt able to accept. In six short verses, she described her confusion and inadequacy on one hand, and the sense of forgiveness and acceptance that she now knew God offered her on the other. Her weakness was to be a blessing, for when the poem was published it was immediately recognised as expressing something many people had felt, but had not been able to say. Also, it raised a huge sum of money, far in excess of that made by the bazaar, for her brother's new school.

Once, when exploring new locations for *Songs of Praise*, I visited the church in Brighton where Charlotte Elliott is now commemorated in a window. St Mary's,

> Just as I am, without one plea
> but that thy blood was shed for me,
> and that thou bidst me come to thee,
> O Lamb of God, I come.
>
> Just as I am, though tossed about
> with many a conflict, many a doubt,
> fightings and fears within, without,
> O Lamb of God, I come.
>
> Just as I am, poor, wretched, blind;
> sight, riches, healing of the mind,
> yea all I need, in thee to find,
> O Lamb of God, I come.
>
> Just as I am, thou wilt receive,
> wilt welcome, pardon, cleanse, relieve:
> because thy promise I believe,
> O Lamb of God, I come.
>
> Just as I am (thy love unknown
> has broken every barrier down),
> now to be thine, yea thine alone,
> O Lamb of God, I come.
>
> Just as I am, of that free love
> the breadth, length, depth and height to prove,
> here for a season, then above,
> O Lamb of God, I come.

Kemp Town, next door to the now-demolished vicarage where the hymn was written, rose in high Victorian splendour after her death in 1871. By the 1980s, however, it had fallen on hard times and its future looked grim. While her brother's school, St Mary's Hall, had gone from strength to strength, the church building seemed to have developed Charlotte's sickness.

Twenty years on, the current vicar, Father Nigel Mason, believes there is new hope for St Mary's. The church is 'acoustically beautiful' and has much to offer music-lovers as well as worshippers. Art exhibitions have been held there, and the new chairlift allows people with physical disabilities to come in to see the magnificent interior, which contrasts with what Father Mason calls its 'tired red-brick exterior'. The doors are kept open as much as possible, and the vicar has taken to listening to Radio 3's *Choral Evensong* when he is in the church, sharing it with parishioners and strangers

Charlotte Elliott.

alike. 'Slowly, slowly,' he says, 'we are discovering what the building has to offer.'

While St Mary's Church is in the Catholic Christian tradition, Charlotte's own faith was closer to that of the great reformer John Calvin, which explains why 'Just as I am, without one plea' played such a key part in Billy Graham's rallies of the 1950s. For many people, the hymn made the point when Graham called people to come up out of their seats an unforgettable emotional experience. There was even a newspaper campaign claiming that the hymn was 'hyping people up', so Graham decided that 'it should only be sung at the call if he felt the need'. Ruth Pashley, a *Songs of Praise* enthusiast, remembers coming up by coach from Margate to hear Billy Graham, and even remembers where her seat was in London's Harringay Arena. She had hoped to hear the choir sing 'Just as I am', but found that it was not to be. Ruth had to wait until Graham's mission of 1984 to hear a choir of 3,000, which included her husband Trevor, singing the hymn. A lady called Kath was in the same choir, and she wrote to Thora Hird on *Praise Be!* to say that the hymn had made her evening. Perhaps that was the same night that Derek, who had also written to Thora, heard it sung. Writing to *Songs of Praise*, he said it was 'the moment I became a Christian'.

Charlotte Elliott's words continue to express the feelings of generations of Christians.

Lord, for the years

Words by Timothy Dudley-Smith (b. 1926)

Tune: 'Lord of the Years' by Michael Baughen (b. 1930)

18

I had the great pleasure of hearing the story of the creation of 'Lord, for the years' from Timothy Dudley-Smith himself: 'I wrote it on a train when I was very pressed for time. I'm thankful if something I write gets picked up, but I suspect anyone who does something in a rush later regrets that they didn't find time to apply the sandpaper a bit more!' He had no idea that he could write hymns: 'When I was first asked by an editor, I said, "No, I can't."' But he did reveal to them that he had written a poem, whose words were based on the Magnificat. This is now the famous and popular hymn 'Tell out, my soul, the greatness of the Lord'.

In February 1967, Dudley-Smith, the now-retired Bishop of Thetford, was asked to write a hymn for the centenary service of the Children's Special Service Mission, now Scripture Union, in St Paul's Cathedral. He was asked to write words that could be fitted to Jean Sibelius's 'Finlandia', as it was to be accompanied by an orchestra who had this tune in their repertoire. So Dudley-Smith wrote 'Lord, for the years'.

It must have sounded very different from today, as we now sing it to a lively tune written by another bishop, Michael Baughen. Dudley-Smith was also later asked to write an extra verse for the Queen's golden jubilee. 'I fear it's a new patch on an old garment,' he said modestly.

'I felt very lonely, but uplifted by the support and prayers of so many people all around me.' Archbishop George Carey used these words to describe his feelings after climbing the ancient steps in Canterbury Cathedral to kneel alone at the altar, and sit for the first time in St Augustine's chair as its 103rd occupant. He was speaking a few days after his enthronement in spring 1991, on a special *Songs of Praise* for which he chose and talked about his favourite hymn. It is easy to understand why a man taking on such a great and lonely responsibility would gain strength from this hymn. The words are all about the love of God that supports and guides and cheers.

In 1991, George Carey was not well known. He had only been a bishop in the Bath and Wells diocese for three years before he was summoned to Canterbury.

Lord, for the years your love has kept and guided,
  urged and inspired us, cheered us on our way,
sought us and saved us, pardoned and provided,
  Lord of the years, we bring our thanks today.

Lord, for that word, the word of life which fires us,
  speaks to our hearts and sets our souls ablaze,
teaches and trains, rebukes us and inspires us,
  Lord of the word, receive your people's praise.

Lord, for our hopes, the dreams of all our living,
  Christ and his kingdom one united aim;
rulers and peoples bound in high thanksgiving,
  Lord of our hopes, our trust is in your Name.*

Lord, for our land, in this our generation,
  spirits oppressed by pleasure, wealth and care;
for young and old, for commonwealth and nation,
  Lord of our land, be pleased to hear our prayer.

Lord, for our world; when we disown and doubt him,
  loveless in strength, and comfortless in pain;
hungry and helpless, lost indeed without him,
  Lord of the world, we pray that Christ may reign.

Lord, for ourselves; in living power remake us,
  self on the cross and Christ upon the throne;
past put behind us, for the future take us,
  Lord of our lives, to live for Christ alone.

* new verse added to commemorate the golden jubilee of Her Majesty the Queen

'Lord of the world, we pray that Christ may reign.' Mealtime at a child-rescue centre in Burundi.

TV reports had emphasised his humble origins as the son of a hospital porter, and the *Songs of Praise* cameras followed him as he revisited Dagenham, where he grew up. 'He's an Arsenal fan, so I've come to pay my respects!' said one young man in the crowd outside Canterbury Cathedral on the day Carey was enthroned.

'The church is light years from many of the people that I grew up with,' said the archbishop in his first sermon. 'Woe to us if we preach religion instead of the gospel – that earthed gospel that takes us directly into the market place of the world.'

At the end of his enthronement service, Carey put this thought into practice. He blessed first his fellow church leaders, and then the huge congregation in the nave, and he did not forget to go to the crowds outside.

It was as he walked down the cathedral, surrounded by pomp and ceremony, that viewers first saw him singing his favourite hymn. He had also chosen it for his consecration as the Bishop of Bath and Wells, and in Canterbury, the archbishop sang it from memory as he passed his wife and family who were enthusiastically joining in.

Dudley-Smith admits that he is 'totally unmusical', but in collaboration with his friend Michael Baughen, his hymn has comfortably made the top forty. Like many of the newer hymns, it has become a nation's favourite through broadcasting, and in particular from being heard so often on *Songs of Praise*. For the millions of viewers who watch TV and who are part of that 'market place' where Carey said the gospel is earthed, the message of Dudley-Smith's hymn has made its mark.

Lord Jesus Christ

(LIVING LORD)

Words by Patrick Appleford (b. 1925)

Tune: 'Living Lord' by Patrick Appleford

28

Lord Jesus Christ,
  you have come to us,
  you are one with us,
    Mary's Son.
Cleansing our souls from all their sin,
pouring your love and goodness in,
Jesus our love for you we sing,
  living Lord.

Lord Jesus Christ,
  now and every day
  teach us how to pray,
    Son of God.
You have commanded us to do
this in remembrance, Lord, of you;
into our lives your power breaks through,
  living Lord.

Lord Jesus Christ,
  you have come to us,
  born as one of us,
    Mary's Son.
Led out to die on Calvary,
risen from death to set us free,
living Lord Jesus, help us see
  you are Lord.

Lord Jesus Christ,
  I would come to you,
  live my life for you,
    Son of God.
All your commands I know are true,
your many gifts will make me new,
into my life your power breaks through,
  living Lord.

'Cliff Richard was singing "Living Doll" at the time, and I thought why not "Living Lord"?'

In 1959, Patrick Appleford was one of six curates serving in the parish of All Saints, Poplar, in London's East End. All Saints still stands: an imposing church whose exterior is reminiscent of St Martin-in-the-Fields. Although the church interior was given a makeover in the 1950s, Canon Appleford remembers a very conservative Church of England at that time. A new Bible in modern English was only used for private reading. But he himself wanted to make connections between the formal worship of All Saints and the people who came along to the church youth club. 'I wanted to help them see not a dead hero, but a living Lord.'

Appleford sat at the piano in his top-floor room in the vicarage, and composed five pieces of music for parish communion that reflected the Catholic tradition

Mass at St Joseph's Catholic church.

of All Saints. 'Ours was one of the first congregations where the service was not just in the hands of the priest and the servers. The people in the pews were becoming more involved in the worship.' 'Living Lord' broke out of the choir mould, and had a unison setting for the whole congregation to sing as a communion hymn. Their Searchlight music group broke new ground with hymns like 'O Lord, all the world belongs to you', which allowed the singer 'to talk to Jesus naturally'.

'Living Lord' is the only one of the five pieces to have survived, and although Appleford has been a successful and prolific composer for many years since, his original communion hymn is still the choice for *Songs of Praise*.

'It was an "early" Appleford,' says the composer, 'but I still get many moving letters about it. One *Songs of Praise* viewer wrote to tell me how much the line "Into our lives, your power breaks through" had helped them cope with a tragedy. The test, I think, of a successful hymn is that it allows people to make it their own.'

Over its forty-year history, *Songs of Praise* has regularly included 'Living Lord'. In the 1960s, the hymn was thoroughly modern, and chosen by producers to illustrate the new face of church music. The composer says, rather ruefully, that another new tune of the time, 'Gracias', to which 'Now thank we all our God' is sung, and which was composed by his colleague and mentor, the late Geoffrey Beaumont, is now described as the 'old' tune.

Appleford's hymn seems to have emerged at an ideal moment. In May 1962, crowds queued for hours to get their first glimpse of Basil Spence's new cathedral in Coventry, which had risen from the ashes of a medieval building destroyed in the war. It was a symbol of reconciliation, and for budding architects like myself, a new and inviting face of Christianity, personified in Graham Sutherland's tapestry of *Christ in Glory*, which dominates the interior. At the parish communion, instead of witnessing a distant formality, we shared the experience, singing together what the composer calls his 'beat ballad' as we came to the altar. The young generation (and I was one) felt welcomed for the first time.

Although he is now retired, Appleford is still composing, and still leading worship. 'What people sing is what they will remember,' he says, and adds, 'What they remember is what they do.'

Coventry Cathedral, old and new.

Lord of all hopefulness, Lord of all joy

Words by Jan Struther (Joyce Placzek) (1901–53)

Tune: 'Slane' (Irish traditional melody)

29

The life and times of the fictional Mrs Miniver were the subjects of Jan Struther's most famous stories. Published in 1939, they formed the basis of a Hollywood film made during the Second World War, which starred Greer Garson and Walter Pigeon. Mrs Miniver's quiet courage and fortitude are said to have helped persuade President Roosevelt that the USA should come to Britain's aid in the war.

Struther was born in London. She changed her name to Jan from Joyce while living in New York, where she promoted her book and the film during the war. As a regular contributor of light verse to magazines, she

Lord of all hopefulness, Lord of all joy,
whose trust, ever child-like, no cares could destroy,
be there at our waking, and give us, we pray,
your bliss in our hearts, Lord, at the break of the day.

Lord of all eagerness, Lord of all faith,
whose strong hands were skilled at the plane and the lathe,
be there at our labours, and give us, we pray,
your strength in our hearts, Lord, at the noon of the day.

Lord of all kindliness, Lord of all grace,
your hands swift to welcome, your arms to embrace,
be there at our homing, and give us, we pray,
your love in our hearts, Lord, at the eve of the day.

Lord of all gentleness, Lord of all calm,
whose voice is contentment, whose presence is balm,
be there at our sleeping, and give us, we pray,
your peace in our hearts, Lord, at the end of the day.

attracted the attention of Percy Dearmer, a London cleric who was editing the words for a new hymn book. The book, *Songs of Praise*, was published in 1925, long before its television counterpart was even dreamed of. Dearmer had an instinct for identifying young talent and had already employed the young Ralph Vaughan Williams as music editor. He asked Struther to write twelve hymns. Believing that she could turn her hand to anything, she accepted, but many heated theological arguments followed before she and her editor agreed the final texts.

One of her twelve hymns is still chosen now and again by children for *Songs of Praise*: 'When a knight won his spurs in the stories of old'. She wrote it to fit a tune called 'Stowey' that Vaughan Williams liked, one of many folk tunes collected from the English countryside by Cecil Sharp. And Struther's hymn 'Lord of all hopefulness, Lord of all joy' still finds its way into the nation's top-forty favourites. It is best known sung to the traditional Irish tune 'Slane', which was arranged by Martin Shaw for *Songs of Praise*. A tune called 'Miniver' has also been composed for the words, but not achieved the same popularity.

Later in life, Struther enjoyed visiting the Berkshire Downs above Goring and Streatley, two proudly independent Doomsday villages linked by a bridge over the Thames. To celebrate Easter 1986, *Songs of Praise* united choirs from the two villages down

by the riverside. The scene was reminiscent of the moment in the Hollywood film *Mrs Miniver*, when everyone assembled on the banks to watch the little ships set off for Dunkirk.

It required something of the Dunkirk spirit to take part in the programme, which was pre-recorded in the summer of 1985, during two days of sunshine that were punctuated by thunderstorms and pouring rain, and complicated by the decision of the local churches that the hymns should be sung on both sides of the river. Everyone tramped over the wet bridge halfway through the recording. If Struther had been alive that day, she could perhaps have suggested another of her twelve hymns, 'O saint of summer, what can we sing for you?', to call down the aid of St Bartholomew.

Struther's daughter, Janet Rance, was among local residents of Goring and Streatley who talked to Roger Royle. She remembered her mother's tremendously eager and zestful approach to life, her 'million hobbies' and her love of botany, which had attracted her to the Berkshire Downs. Wild flowers were best. Janet said, 'The last thing she was looking at as she died was a most wonderful bunch of roses.'

Displaying the fortitude of Mrs Miniver and the radiant energy she had described in her mother, Janet also talked about her own battle with cancer: 'I've realised how precious every moment is. I used to moan about the rainy days, but now I realise their value.' This seemed to be summed up best in her mother's hymn, 'Lord of all hopefulness', but this had already been chosen by someone else for the same programme, as had 'When a knight won his spurs', so Janet instead chose her mother's own favourite hymn. This was 'O world invisible', a setting of 'The kingdom of God', the poem by Francis Thompson. As so often on *Songs of Praise*, 'O world invisible' sung on that stormy summer's afternoon by the River Thames expressed, through poetry of camera shot and word, all our human lifetime's search for the ever-elusive truth:

Yea, in the night, my soul, my daughter,
  cry – clinging heaven by the hems;
and lo, Christ walking on the water
  not of Gennesareth, but Thames!

Lord, the light of your love is shining

(SHINE, JESUS, SHINE)

Words by Graham Kendrick (b. 1950)

Tune: 'Shine, Jesus, Shine' by Graham Kendrick

20

How does a new song find its way not just into the top forty, but into the top twenty of the nation's favourites, joining the centuries-old crown jewels of great hymnody?

Graham Kendrick, whose songs have travelled around the world, grew up in suburban London in the 1960s, the decade that began with the building of the Berlin Wall and the Cold War at its worst. But other barriers were coming down, and the BBC's *Light Programme*, with its demure music, was being stormed by the new pop 'pirate' radio stations. 1967 saw the birth of Radio 1, and in 1961 there was another instant smash hit: the BBC's *Songs of Praise*.

According to Kendrick, the recipe for his success began with growing up listening to The Beatles, alongside singing hymns from the *Baptist Hymn Book*. Like many of his generation, Kendrick, one of our most popular Christian songwriters, found a way to enjoy both worlds. On Sunday nights, having gained parental approval by going, hymn book in hand, to church, he would listen under the bedclothes to a transistor radio – to the exciting sound of John, Paul, George and Ringo being played by the pirate disc-jockeys on the high seas. And he made a discovery: he had a natural ear for music.

By his own admission, the singer and composer's voice has a limited range. But that has not been a disadvantage, and in fact is the very reason why many of his worship songs are so popular. He knows that if he finds a tune easy to sing, then so will most people.

'Shine, Jesus, Shine' emerged by trial and error, as Kendrick experimented with different chords on his guitar. At first the verses, beginning 'Lord, the light of your love is shining', were sung without any chorus. Then, whether it was the instinct of a good musician, or, as he believes, God's inspiration, the chorus 'Shine, Jesus, shine' came to him. Almost eerily echoing the experience of many famous hymn-writers, it was all written down and the music completed in just thirty minutes. The chorus had supplied the magic ingredient.

Kendrick admits that when he first tried out the complete song at events like Spring Harvest, even he was amazed at how quickly it took off. Huge crowds picked up the verses as well as the chorus. It was soon being sung everywhere, in living rooms and mission chapels, in football stadiums and even in great cathedrals.

On a spring day in 1988, the Church of England launched the Church Urban Fund to support hard-pressed people of the inner cities. The great and the good gathered in Westminster Abbey. Solemn

---

Lord, the light of your love is shining,
in the midst of the darkness, shining:
Jesus, light of the world, shine upon us;
set us free by the truth you now bring us –
  shine on me, shine on me.

Shine, Jesus, shine,
fill this land with the Father's glory;
blaze, Spirit, blaze,
set our hearts on fire.
Flow, river, flow,
flood the nations with grace and mercy;
send forth your word, Lord,
and let there be light!

Lord, I come to your awesome presence,
from the shadows into your radiance;
by the blood I may enter your brightness:
search me, try me, consume all my darkness –
  shine on me, shine on me.

As we gaze on your kingly brightness
so our faces display your likeness,
ever changing from glory to glory:
mirrored here, may our lives tell your story –
  shine on me, shine on me.

processions of vergers and clergy were followed by solemn prayers of dedication. Near the end, the atmosphere lightened. Led, gently at first, by a small worship group from a parish that the fund aimed to benefit, they began to sing 'Shine, Jesus, Shine'. The tune's infectious spirit quickly spread to every historic corner of the ancient abbey where kings and queens have been crowned, and poets and statesmen are buried. The midday sun suddenly seemed to break through the stained glass. Any trace of established-church pomposity fell away under the influence of the joyful singers – like the ones from the Manchester diocese, who were led by their own bishop, the late Stanley Booth Clibborn, who was dressed not in robes

but in an old, battered raincoat. The leaders of industry and business, who had come to mark their great act of charity, learned a new song from people from one of England's poorest dioceses. Bursting with energy and faith, they provided the greatest blessing the fund could have hoped for.

After thousands of performances of his song by millions of singers around the world, Kendrick stood alone with his guitar on the stage of the Royal Albert Hall for the first *Songs of Praise* of 2002. 'Join me, do,' he called out to the full house, as if it was the song's very first performance. And how they did, and have continued to do, and will do for years to come.

Love divine, all loves excelling

Words by Charles Wesley (1707–88)

Tunes: 'Blaenwern' by W.P. Rowlands (1860–1937); 'Love Divine' by John Stainer (1840–1901)

8

'I am sure, even now, I could take you to the exact seat in our Methodist church in Stockport where I received my call to the ministry. And I remember the exact moment: we were all singing "Love divine, all loves excelling".'

This is how the most popular Wesley hymn in the top forty became a memory to cherish for the Reverend Rosemary Wakelin. After the service, she told her mother, who sighed, 'Oh my darling, they don't have ladies for ministers!'

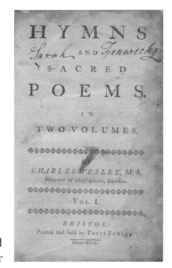

Charles Wesley's Hymns and Sacred Poems in Two Volumes *from 1749.*

'Well, of course, I did have to wait a bit, and anyway I was only seven years old! But I am eternally grateful to Charles Wesley; he's like a spiritual godfather to me.'

Now a Methodist minister, Rosemary was also a religious broadcaster, long before her son, Michael Wakelin, the present series producer of *Songs of Praise*, chose his career in radio and television production. Michael benefits from his mother's encyclopedic knowledge of her spiritual godfather's life and work, and her capacity for repeating from heart the words of all the Wesley hymns. She even knows their number in the *Methodist Hymn Book*. She shares this peculiar talent with Ray Short, a Methodist minister and the first series producer of *Songs of Praise*. I think it must be a Methodist thing.

In Wesley's time, it was as common for Methodists to carry a small pocket volume of his hymns as it is for

people today to carry a wallet of credit cards. The eighteenth-century *Methodist Magazine* devotes many pages to stories of Christians on their deathbeds for whom hymns were painkillers. One Mrs Crane of Preston, who was seemingly at death's door, greeted a bedside visitor with the words 'Sit down by me and help me to sing,' and then 'broke forth in singing in a kind of ecstasy of delight'. Nine days later, 'her breath cut shorter', she implored a friend to 'Shout his praise – I can't wait to shout his praise,' bringing to an end her days, which had been filled with the poetry of the Wesleys. Mrs Hutton of Sunderland, 'a steady and useful member of the Methodist Society', came to the end of her life with Charles Wesley's two volumes of hymns at her side. Time after time, her minister, Mr Benson, had been amazed to find her rallying by reciting Wesley's verse.

These published accounts helped to further increase the popularity of Methodism. Similarly, *Songs of Praise* interviews have revealed that hymns sometimes play a surprisingly important part in people's lives. I often wonder if a TV programme that shows other people singing, many of whose viewers cannot sing a note of music themselves, could have been a success for over forty years without the Wesleys.

For their wedding, Bronwen Douse and her fiancé chose 'Love divine, all loves excelling'. The last verse, and the last two lines in particular, still sum up the faith that helped see them through some very dark days. In 1982, midwife Bronwen spent ninety-three of the most frightening days of her life – in the Falkland Islands. Immediately after the Argentinian invasion, she continued to worship in the little Anglican cathedral in Port Stanley, until the Argentinians enforced a curfew. At first, they still could reach the Catholic church, but as the British task force fought its way into Port Stanley, the friendly fire of the rescuers became as terrifying and dangerous as any enemy action. Bronwen remembers delivering a baby whose future home was being destroyed in the allied assault. 'But we could just get out to the shop nearby, and it sort of became our "church". Each morning, we'd meet there and hug each other, thankful that we were still alive.'

Love divine, all loves excelling,
  joy of heaven to earth come down,
fix in us thy humble dwelling,
  all thy faithful mercies crown.
Jesu, thou art all compassion,
  pure, unbounded love thou art;
visit us with thy salvation,
  enter every trembling heart.

Come, almighty to deliver,
  let us all thy life receive;
suddenly return, and never,
  never more thy temples leave.
Thee we would be always blessing,
  serve thee as thy hosts above,
pray, and praise thee, without ceasing,
  glory in thy perfect love.

Finish then thy new creation,
  pure and sinless let us be;
let us see thy great salvation,
  perfectly restored in thee;
changed from glory into glory,
  till in heaven we take our place,
till we cast our crowns before thee,
  lost in wonder, love and praise.

Make me a channel of your peace

Words from a prayer attributed to St Francis of Assisi (1182–1226)

Tune: 'Channel of Peace' by Sebastian Temple (b. 1928)

7

St Francis of Assisi, although he was born in twelfth-century Italy, seems strangely like a man of our own times. The best known and best loved of all the saints, he seems thoroughly contemporary in his love for animals and the natural world. His compassion for the outcast also seems ahead of its time. He responded in a Christlike way to the harsh and hierarchical life of medieval Europe. He founded the Franciscans, an order dedicated to serving the poor and respecting the whole of God's creation. His itinerant friars in their brown habits are still to be seen on today's city streets. If our consciences are troubled by today's men and women who take Franciscan vows of poverty, chastity and obedience, and put their prayers into action by serving the poor, then we are in touch with the upside-down life of St Francis.

The son of a rich cloth merchant in Assisi, the

young Francis was gallant, generous and high spirited. When he was twenty, he was thrown into prison for some months, after being caught up in a border dispute. When he was eventually freed, he became dissatisfied with his worldly life. During a serious illness, he began to feel that God was calling him to something new. He went on a pilgrimage to Rome, where he was soon quite literally giving all his money and even his clothes away to the beggars. Then he became a beggar himself. He discovered first-hand both the hardships and the joys of poverty, and drew up a simple Rule by which to live. His father disowned him, but he had found happiness for the first time.

Over the centuries since then, thousands have taken up the Franciscan way of life, and millions of Christians have wished that they could better follow St Francis's example. Today, there are Franciscans working all around the world, and even on the glamorous West Coast of America, they maintain their simple lifestyle. All along the Californian coastline is a chain of eighteenth-century mission churches, many with cloisters built in the medieval style of the monastery at St Damiano in Assisi that St Francis helped restore when he started his order.

The work to build on St Francis's original vision still goes on. It was an unfulfilled dream of the late Harry Secombe to make a programme about these mission churches, and to sing St Francis's prayer there.

'The way things are right now, if the words of St Francis in this hymn were taken to heart, the world would be a much better place.' So said Daniel O'Donnell before singing 'Make me a channel of your peace' in a recent celebration of forty years of *Songs of Praise* at the Royal Albert Hall. 'You express yourself differently when you sing a hymn,' he told Aled Jones with beguiling simplicity. Compared with other types of music, he continued, 'It gets the inner self out more.'

Make me a channel of your peace.
Where there is hatred, let me bring your love.
Where there is injury, your pardon, Lord,
and where there's doubt, true faith in you.

Make me a channel of your peace.
Where there's despair in life, let me bring hope.
Where there is darkness only light,
and where there's sadness ever joy.

O Master, grant that I may never seek
so much to be consoled as to console,
to be understood as to understand,
to be loved, as to love, with all my soul.

Make me a channel of your peace.
It is in pardoning that we are pardoned,
in giving of ourselves that we receive,
and in dying that we're born to eternal life.

Here are St Francis's own words, from his Rule:

I counsel, admonish and exhort my brothers in the Lord
Jesus Christ not to quarrel or argue or judge others when
they go about in the world; but let them be meek, peaceful,
modest, gentle and humble, speaking courteously to
everyone, as is becoming. They should not ride horseback
unless they are compelled by an obvious need or infirmity.

Into whatever house they enter, let them first say,
'Peace be to this house!'

St Francis receives the stigmata.

Morning has broken

Words by Eleanor Farjeon (1881–1965)

Tune: 'Bunessan' (Gaelic melody)

36

One day in the 1970s, Cat Stevens was sharing a recording session with rock musician Rick Wakeman. With a minute to fill, Stevens asked Wakeman to play something on his keyboard, and he picked out the opening lines of an old hymn tune. 'Play me some more,' said the pop singer, famous for many hits in the 1960s and 1970s, including 'Matthew and Son' and 'Moonshadow'. Wakeman responded with more. 'More,' said Stevens, until Wakeman had played the whole tune, and more than a mere gap in a session had been filled. Stevens had found a song that was to become one of his biggest hits.

These days, Stevens, who was brought up in a Greek Orthodox family and educated at a Catholic school, is a strict Muslim, and goes by the name of Yusuf Islam. However, his chance partnership with Wakeman resulted in huge popularity for a once little-known hymn and an old Gaelic melody.

A recent review posted on the Cat Stevens website describes the impact. The writer of the review recalls religious instruction at school in the 1970s, which was taken by the vicar. The vicar insisted that 'Morning has broken', at the time a hit record, was not 'proper' religion. 'Sorry, Padre,' ends the reviewer. 'In twenty-five years, it has lasted longer and been of more significance than anything you had to say!'

Some songs easily cross over from one world to another. Simon and Garfunkel's 1970 hit 'Bridge Over Troubled Water' has travelled in the opposite direction from 'Morning has broken', and is now regularly chosen for *Songs of Praise*, especially when the location is Northern Ireland. Another classic example is 'You'll Never Walk Alone', originally a hit for Gerry and the Pacemakers in the 1960s, which was sung by a grieving community after the Hillsborough football stadium disaster, and is now included in the *BBC Songs of Praise* hymn book, the only entry from Oscar Hammerstein.

John Bell, a hymn-writer and compiler, says that such songs cross over because, like country-and-western music, they sometimes have the best words to help us deal with the dark side of life. 'When the church doesn't supply such songs, then the secular songs will have to do, if we are to express our grief,' he says.

'Bunessan', the tune always associated with Farjeon's hymn, comes from a Gaelic collection published in 1900, *Macbean's Songs and Hymns of the Gael*. The tune is named after a tiny village on the Ross of Mull, part of the huge island off the west

Morning has broken
  like the first morning,
blackbird has spoken
  like the first bird.
Praise for the singing,
  praise for the morning,
praise for them, springing
  fresh from the Word!

Sweet the rain's new fall
  sunlit from heaven,
like the first dewfall
  on the first grass.
Praise for the sweetness
  of the wet garden,
sprung in completeness
  where his feet pass.

Mine is the sunlight;
  mine is the morning,
born of the one light
  Eden saw play!
Praise with elation,
  praise every morning,
God's re-creation
  of the new day!

coast of Scotland, across which pilgrims must travel to reach the tiny island of Iona.

In 1881, when visitors were rare, the census recorded that three-quarters of the people of Bunessan were Gaelic-speakers. Today's visitors come from all over the world to stay in the abbey and share the simple hospitality of the Iona Community. They can best share the experience described in the hymn by leaving Iona on the dawn ferry and joining the road to Bunessan. The summer sun rises over Ben More, and the waters of Loch Scridain glitter and flash. To the north, giant cliffs are home to eagles. Even though a Highland summer dawn usually resounds with what my fisherman priest friend calls 'the music of wind and rain and midge', they will be in a place as close as any on earth to the Garden of Eden described by Farjeon in her hymn. And it is as fresh and exciting as on that first morning.

My song is love unknown

Words by Samuel Crossman (1624–83/84)

Tune: 'Love Unknown' by John Ireland (1879–1962)

30

Once upon a time, a series producer of *Songs of Praise* persuaded the faithful vergers of Wells Cathedral to clear all the chairs out of the huge nave. The result revealed how a medieval church would have looked, with a vast open space in the middle and just stone ledges around the edges where the 'weakest could go to the wall'. It was only the beginning of the plan, for TV cameras were positioned to record the moment when the great west doors would swing open, revealing a small donkey carrying a young man wearing the garb of first-century Palestine. Led by the donkey and its rider, hundreds of children waving palm branches and singing Palm Sunday hymns would then flood into the nave.

Long afterwards, this remained a highlight for viewers, who pleaded with Thora Hird to show the donkey again and again on *Praise Be!* From that day on, whenever Thora chose hymns for Palm Sunday, she would always try to include the donkey at Wells Cathedral, and would always include, in one version or another, 'My song is love unknown', which has long been one of the nation's favourite hymns.

It is also the favourite hymn of Hugh Faupel, the present editor of *Songs of Praise*: 'It takes some beating, and it can be done wonderfully, either as a single voice or through a large, solid sound coming from a huge congregation.'

Samuel Crossman published 'My song is love unknown' as a poem in 1664, but it then disappeared for over 200 years, and did not reappear until 1868. The words describe, in sweet, simple and direct language, the coming of God to earth in the form of Jesus, and then, verse by verse, the story of his passion and death. 'Sometimes they strew his way, and his sweet praises sing,' describes Jesus' entry into Jerusalem on a donkey, the scene re-enacted in *Songs of Praise* at Wells Cathedral.

But in Crossman's own time, all the dramatic rituals of the pre-Reformation church during Holy Week were

My song is love unknown,
  my Saviour's love to me,
love to the loveless shown,
  that they might lovely be.
    O, who am I,
      that for my sake
      my Lord should take
    frail flesh, and die?

He came from his blest throne,
  salvation to bestow:
but men made strange, and none
  the longed-for Christ would know.
    But O, my friend,
      my friend indeed,
      who at my need
    his life did spend!

Sometimes they strew his way,
  and his sweet praises sing;
resounding all the day
  hosannas to their King.
    Then 'Crucify!'
      is all their breath,
      and for his death
    they thirst and cry.

Why, what hath my Lord done?
  What makes this rage and spite?
He made the lame to run,
  he gave the blind their sight.
    Sweet injuries!
      Yet they at these
      themselves displease,
    and 'gainst him rise.

They rise, and needs will have
  my dear Lord made away;
a murderer they save,
  the Prince of Life they slay.
    Yet cheerful he
      to suffering goes,
      that he his foes
    from thence might free.

Here might I stay and sing,
  no story so divine;
never was love, dear King,
  never was grief like thine!
    This is my friend,
      in whose sweet praise
      I all my days
    could gladly spend.

thought of as idolatrous by the reformers. In some churches, Palm Sunday was marked by the appearance of the Palmesel, a huge, wheel-mounted, wooden carving of Christ on a donkey. The plague of 1665 and the great fire of London the following year were seen by the Puritans as God's judgment on centuries of idolatry and disobedience.

Just before he died, Crossman was made Dean of Bristol. This came at the end of a violent chapter in British history, what with the English civil war and the Monmouth rebellion, and after centuries of religious upheaval. Crossman himself had been ejected from his Suffolk parish in 1662 because he had expressed horror at the execution of King Charles I.

Pioneer religious broadcaster Dick Sheppard had the theme of Crossman's hymn in mind when he wrote his autobiography, *The Impatience of a Parson*, in 1928, for his experience was indeed of 'love unknown'. The title refers to his impatience for the day when all churches would unite to sing of the love of God. He ends his book: 'If we will not strive to this end, then Christ must be crucified afresh, and it will be the lot of some other civilisation to assist in his inevitable resurrection.'

Love was always the theme of the Sunday-evening sermons he broadcast to millions of crystal-set listeners in the 1920s. Sheppard was persuaded, like the vergers who had cleared the chairs from Wells Cathedral, to take the risk of working with the media. Once or twice, he even held a special service in the Royal Albert Hall, where he could meet his listeners face to face. Incurably unparsonical, he once described what it was like to be a Christian: 'You're a marked man for life.'

O Jesus, I have promised

Words by John Ernest Bode (1816–74)

Many tunes

22

The Reverend John Bode published *Hymns for the Gospel of the Day for Each Sunday and Festival of Our Lord* in 1860. Only one hymn, which he wrote for a children's confirmation service, has survived from that collection: 'O Jesus, I have promised'. But *Songs of Praise* choirs are spoilt for choice over which tune to sing it to. The *BBC Songs of Praise* book lists: 'Wolvercote', 'Day of Rest' and 'Hatherop Castle'. Other hymn books include 'Meirionydd', 'Missionary Hymn', 'Bremen' and 'Thornbury'.

Woe betide the producer who chooses the 'wrong' tune. Everyone, both in participating choirs and in the viewing audience, knows that there is a 'right' tune and a 'wrong' tune, but each of them will have a different idea of what that is. To the non-musical hymn-lover, 'Thornbury' is sometimes confused with 'Wolvercote'. If those two do sound slightly similar, there is no difficulty in distinguishing the jaunty 'Hatherop Castle', written by Geoffrey Beaumont in the 1960s. This is the 'new' tune, which for some viewers is associated with a fresh, young-people-friendly church that welcomed them to membership. For others, this is quite definitely the 'wrong' tune, usurping the older 'right' tunes. When I was series producer of *Songs of Praise*, one viewer, campaigning for 'Wolvercote', warned me that if 'Hatherop Castle' was ever again used for 'O Jesus, I have promised', they would disrupt the programme by banging the church doors until the choirs came to their senses. As far as I know, they have not yet carried out the threat.

Action is the theme of Bode's intensely personal prayer of self-dedication. I cannot remember which tune was used in the late 1970s, when *Songs of Praise* went to the Camberwell citadel of the Salvation Army. 'O Jesus, I have promised' was chosen by a young couple who were finishing their training at the nearby staff college in Denmark Hill. It was the hymn that

Catherine Bramwell-Booth and her mother, Mrs Bramwell-Booth, leading the procession to the site of the first Salvation Army women's shelter in London in 1934.

O Jesus, I have promised
  to serve thee to the end;
be thou for ever near me,
  my master and my friend:
I shall not fear the battle
  if thou art by my side,
nor wander from the pathway
  if thou wilt be my guide.

O let me hear thee speaking
  in accents clear and still,
above the storms of passion,
  the murmurs of self-will;
O speak to reassure me,
  to hasten, or control;
O speak, and make me listen,
  thou guardian of my soul.

O Jesus, thou hast promised
  to all who follow thee –
that where thou art in glory
  there shall thy servant be;
and Jesus, I have promised
  to serve thee to the end;
O give me grace to follow,
  my master and my friend.

O let me see thy footmarks,
  and in them plant mine own;
my hope to follow duly
  is in thy strength alone:
O guide me, call me, draw me,
  uphold me to the end;
and then in heaven receive me,
  my Saviour and my friend.

would be used at the special service, when they would be commissioned as Salvationists.

My wife Liz, who was the researcher for this edition, recalls how the effect of the words, combined with the dynamic sound of the Salvation Army band and singers, made her wonder whether she should not be marching out of the BBC and lining up behind the famous flag. To this day, she remembers the warmth and encouragement communicated by the faces of the songsters and the conductor, Norman Beardsall.

The result of promising to serve Jesus to the end of life was at the heart of another famous religious broadcast. In *180 Not Out*, a TV programme from the 1980s, Malcolm Muggeridge was the eighty-year-old stripling interviewing commissioner Catherine Bramwell-Booth as she celebrated her 100th birthday. The grandaughter of William Booth, founder of the Salvation Army, appeared in full uniform, complete with the traditional bonnet, as she turned the tables on her interviewer to scrutinise his much-vaunted Christian faith:

'I'm 80', said Muggeridge, 'and I'm finished.'

'I'm 100', said the commissioner, 'and I'm in love with life – and I want more!'

Bramwell-Booth described how, as a young candidate in training, she felt inadequate: 'I couldn't sing solos and that was one of the requirements. Luckily, I was sent out with a lieutenant with a sweet soprano voice. But you see, ask a crowd of tipsy men in a pub what they want to hear and it's "Tell me the old, old story of Jesus and his love". They are right too; it's a very good story.' As she spoke, she looked closely at Muggeridge, just as the band conductor had once looked at the researcher for *Songs of Praise*. 'You take orders, do as you're told in the Army,' continued its most senior officer, 'but I've faced great difficulty with my faith, as I am by nature a doubting Thomas. You see the glory, the beauty, the joy of life is being able to say every day, "Lord, thy will, not mine be done." If I die and find myself in hell, then I shall go on preaching Christ and then it won't be hell any more.'

O Lord my God, when I in awesome wonder

(HOW GREAT THOU ART)

Words translated by Stuart K. Hine (1899–1989)

Tune: 'How Great Thou Art' by Stuart K. Hine

1

It fell to presenter Aled Jones to announce the nation's favourite hymn before a capacity audience in the Royal Albert Hall on the first Sunday of 2002. He introduced Jonathan Veira to sing 'How Great Thou Art', a hymn for which viewers' votes have continued to pile up, keeping it as their number-one hymn. The letters and emails included one with a memory of an unsurpassed performance in the 1980s, also in the Royal Albert Hall, by a Welsh tenor who was joined by a very popular young boy soprano from Wales – Aled Jones!

Veira paused before singing this famous hymn to explain to Jones why he liked it so much: 'I enjoy singing such a great hymn that takes us away from ourselves and points towards God.' Once, Billy Graham, in a rare comment on a hymn, said much the same, admitting that it had encouraged him to break his rule of letting his choir leader, Cliff Barrows, choose the music for his rallies. 'I urged him to use it as often as possible, because it was such a God-honouring song.'

Songs of Praise conductor Nigel Swinford has what he calls an obsession to scrape the layers of varnish off hymns, like stripping furniture, and enthusiastically researches them to see what they are made of and where they come from. He remembers 'How Great Thou Art' with huge enthusiasm from when it first arrived at youth meetings of the strict Christian Brethren, when he was growing up in the 1950s: 'We sang Stuart Hine's English translation of the Russian words.' Hine, a great evangelist, and his wife had first discovered the hymn in Russia and had sung it, in Russian, as a duet in the 1920s during the course of their missionary work in the communist world. Travelling into the Carpathian Mountains one day, the couple had been caught in a violent storm. The thunder was as awe-inspiring and as mighty as the one they had been singing about. The next day, the storm behind them, they came down the mountain into Romania and reached Bukovina, which means 'the land of the beech tree'. Walking 'through the

> O Lord my God, when I in awesome wonder
>   consider all the works thy hand hath made,
> I see the stars, I hear the mighty thunder,
>   thy power throughout the universe displayed:
>
> *Then sings my soul, my Saviour God, to thee,*
>   *How great thou art, how great thou art!*
> *Then sings my soul, my Saviour God, to thee,*
>   *How great thou art, how great thou art!*
>
> When through the woods and forest glades
>   I wander
>   and hear the birds sing sweetly in the trees;
> when I look down from lofty mountain grandeur,
>   and hear the brook, and feel the gentle breeze;
>
> And when I think that God his Son not sparing,
>   sent him to die – I scarce can take it in,
> that on the cross, my burden gladly bearing,
>   he bled and died to take away my sin:
>
> When Christ shall come with shout of acclamation
>   and take me home – what joy shall fill my heart!
> Then shall I bow in humble adoration,
>   and there proclaim, my God, how great thou art!

woods and forest glades' they found a community that had possessed a Bible for years, but could not read. With Hine's encouragement, one woman learned to read with the aid of this Bible, and slowly the whole village heard the gospel story. Eventually, they all became Christians.

When, after the Second World War, Hine was working on his translation of the hymn into English, he remembered all these sights and experiences and added a fourth verse to offer hope to thousands of refugees then fleeing from the Soviet Union. As he worked on the words, he thought it odd that the original version made no mention of the 'lofty mountain grandeur' that

was so much a part of the Russian landscape, so he added it himself.

Recently, however, Nigel Swinford met someone who remembered Hine's amazement when he first discovered a Swedish poem revealing that 'How Great Thou Art' was not of Russian origin at all. It had migrated from Sweden, a land where there were no lofty mountains, to reach the oppressed people of the Ukraine. Shortly before he died, Englishman James Lees, another evangelist working in Sweden, had uncovered the original version of the hymn. It was a poem of nine verses called '*O store Gud*', and it had been written in 1885 by Carl Boberg, a preacher who went on to serve in the Swedish parliament. Like Hine, Boberg had also experienced a storm followed by a calm, still day in the woods, where a single thrush could be heard singing. Although they never met, both men contributed to a profound hymn that seems to be more than just an all-time favourite.

Swinford says that he never sees the hymn on *Songs of Praise*, when it is usually illustrated with images of mountains and woods, without thinking of the persecuted Christians that Hine prayed with. He himself uses it to pray for the oppressed people of today's world. 'It follows straight on from the direct evangelical style of Moody and Sankey, starting with the creation, but then taking the singer to the cross and then finally to the hope of heaven.' It is no surprise that this powerful hymn tops the list.

O love that wilt not let me go

Words by George Matheson (1842–1906)

Tune: 'St Margaret' by Albert Peace (1844–1912)

9

Standing on the pebble-strewn shore of the Firth of Clyde, on a winter's day in the Argyllshire village of Innellan, I am trying to imagine the Victorian world of the Reverend George Matheson and the scene here in the summer of 1881, when in a moment of intense sadness he wrote a poem called 'O love that wilt not let me go'.

During that summer, paddle steamers packed with trippers called at the pier, which has now vanished. Later that year, the race to tie up and catch new passengers at the pier became so feverish that two MacBrayne steamers, *Sheila* and *Columba*, collided just offshore. A few years earlier, people from Innellan had crammed onto excursion boats that took them 'doon the watter' to Rothesay on the Isle of Bute, where the great Charles Haddon Spurgeon was preaching to a crowd of 20,000 on Jesus healing on the Sabbath. As alcohol was only supplied to 'travellers' on Sundays at the time, it was reported that fighting broke out and 'the effects of a plentiful supply of drink on the return journey were much evident'.

An illustration from Glasgow Illustrated *of the Highland steamer* Columba.

O love that wilt not let me go,
  I rest my weary soul in thee;
I give thee back the life I owe,
that in thine ocean depths its flow
  may richer, fuller be.

O light that followest all my way,
  I yield my flickering torch to thee;
my heart restores its borrowed ray,
that in thy sunshine's blaze its day
  may brighter, fairer be.

O joy that seekest me through pain,
  I cannot close my heart to thee;
I trace the rainbow through the rain,
and feel the promise is not vain
  that morn shall tearless be.

O cross that liftest up my head,
  I dare not ask to fly from thee;
I lay in dust life's glory dead,
and from the ground there blossoms red
  life that shall endless be.

Ian Bradley, a minister of the Church of Scotland, has studied Victorian hymnody and has given us a credible portrait of Matheson, a minister whose legendary tragic love story is almost as familiar to *Songs of Praise* viewers as his hymn. Bradley describes how, when Matheson was eighteen months old, his mother realised that there was a serious problem with his eyesight. By the age of eighteen, he could hardly see at all, but he was popular with fellow students at Glasgow University, where he was academically brilliant, and studyied both arts and divinity. He enjoyed singing and acting, and at the age of just seven, he persuaded his family to be a 'congregation' while he stood on a chair and preached a pretend sermon.

But increasingly, as his eyesight worsened, Matheson had to face life in a dark and often lonely world. However, this isolation led him to develop the remarkable imagination that made him a gifted poet and preacher. His exposition of scripture was very different from Spurgeon's revivalist fervour. Theologically, he was a liberal. He would describe the hard human journey of being committed to the path that leads to God. For Matheson, God was elusive, hidden in shadow, but ever-present, even in the empty wilderness of the Highlands, which sheltered his Innellan parish from the winter storms.

The familiar story is that Matheson's sadness on the day he wrote 'O love that wilt not let me go' was because he had been rejected by the woman he loved. She had declared that she would not give up her life for a blind man. In reality, this probably never happened in such a stark way. The poem emerged on the day that one of his sisters, who had been his housekeeper and close companion, was getting married in Glasgow. Matheson, unable to go to the family celebrations, later described what happened:

'It is the quickest composition I ever achieved. It was done in three minutes. It seemed to me at the time as if someone was dictating the composition to me, and also giving the expression – my hymn was the voice of my depression. It was not made for utilitarian purposes; it was wrung out of my heart.'

Matheson's intensely felt poem has become a hymn whose words seem made for the uncertain mind of the modern world. The writer and broadcaster Ian Mackenzie, also a minister, sees it as 'nakedly about love, with a knock-out ending. To sing it is to go on a journey through writing of the calibre of a Shakespeare sonnet.' Matheson discovers and reveals how Christ's life and death show that, in surrendering to God, we cannot avoid pain, but we will overcome it.

My broadcasting colleague Johnston McKay has discovered that even this fine hymn was censored by the Church authorities of the time. The General Assembly of the Church of Scotland required that if the hymn was to appear in their new hymnal, the original phrase 'I climb the rainbow' must become 'I trace the rainbow through the rain,' since the former was merely imaginative and not possible. They failed to understand the vision of the blind preacher.

Today, on a winter's Sunday, a gusty wind is blowing up the firth from the distant mountains of the Isle of Arran. Crying gulls circle above the waves, and further up the hill in the bare woods, where Innellan Church and Manse still stand, rooks add their raucous tones to the sounds of the receding tide roaring across the pebbled shore. As the congregation sings the hymn, the parish is waiting for a new minister to come and help with an Alpha course. 'Oh yes, ministers are very hard to come by these days,' says a resident.

But down on the shore, opposite where the busy pier once stood, the 'Bits and Bobs' charity shop, run by the church in a portacabin, is a tiny sign that Matheson's vision is not forgotten.

O thou who camest from above

Words by Charles Wesley (1707–88)

Tune: 'Hereford' by Samuel Sebastian Wesley (1810–76)

38

It is perhaps not surprising to discover several links between Charles Wesley, the great Methodist evangelist, and John Robinson, the late Bishop of Woolwich and author of the notorious best-selling book *Honest to God*.

Both men took holy orders in the Church of England, and both created a Christian rumpus that spread far beyond that church. Both were reviled by their mother church, and found themselves in a wilderness. Both are now seen to have led millions of people, if not out of the wilderness, at least into a new understanding of faith. There the similarities might end, except that every stage of Robinson's life – his marriage, his ordination, family baptisms, his consecration as a bishop and his funeral – was marked by the singing of Wesley's hymn 'O thou who camest from above'. Just after the Second World War, he even lived in lodgings near Bristol with two spinster sisters, Irene and Ethel Blackmore, who were directly descended from John Wesley.

In 1963, fewer than two years after the launch of BBC TV's *Songs of Praise*, Robinson, a Cambridge academic who was also an influential pastor, finished a book that he proposed calling *A New Mutation in Christianity*. His wife Ruth said that that was no good at all. Only one title would do it justice: *Honest to God*. Somehow, this title caught the eye of an *Observer* journalist. Their write-up, as Robinson later wrote, 'acted like a tin-opener'.

There was uproar. Tabloid newspapers declared that Robinson intended to destroy the 'faith of simple people' by his suggestion that the nursery view of God as 'daddy in the sky' would not do. He was denounced by other church leaders, sometimes before they had

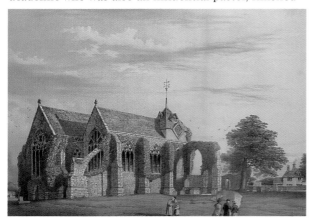

Winchelsea Church, the site of John Wesley's last sermon in October 1790.

O thou who camest from above,
   the pure celestial fire to impart,
kindle a flame of sacred love
   on the mean altar of my heart.

There let it for thy glory burn
   with inextinguishable blaze;
and trembling to its source return,
   in humble prayer, and fervent praise.

Jesus, confirm my heart's desire
   to work, and speak, and think for thee;
still let me guard the holy fire,
   and still stir up thy gift in me:

Ready for all thy perfect will,
   my acts of faith and love repeat,
till death thy endless mercies seal,
   and make my sacrifice complete.

even read the book. But many others thought that *Honest to God* had come at just the right time. One clergyman, in defending Robinson, quoted Jung: '[People] have heard enough about guilt and sin… and want to learn to reconcile themselves with their own nature and to love the enemy in their own hearts. They want to say "yes" to life.'

As the row continued in a less physical, but no less vitriolic, form than that which had surrounded John and Charles Wesley, Nansie Blackie, a theologian, like Robinson, of Yorkshire stock, got to the heart of the matter: 'It is important that this search, these questionings, these understandings are contained within the great traditions of Christian orthodoxy, for no sect, no splinter group has the resources for the tension, freedom and faith required.'

The Wesleys did not wish to found a new church, but their revolutionary preaching of God's free grace was too much for the Anglican Church of the time. So it nearly was in Robinson's case, but this time, in a mass-media age, the hullabaloo was as much due to headlines, rumours and innuendos as to people understanding the book or listening to the bishop. But *Honest to God*, like the hymn that was its author's favourite, became a huge bestseller.

'O thou who camest from above' is a hymn of total dedication, based on a verse in the book of Leviticus: 'The fire shall ever be burning upon the altar, it shall never go out.' John Wesley took particular pleasure in the first two verses of his brother's hymn. Charles Wesley's grandson, Samuel Sebastian Wesley, wrote the tune 'Hereford', which today goes hand in hand with the hymn, although it was not attached to it until 1916, when it appeared in a supplement to *Hymns Ancient and Modern*. Samuel Sebastian Wesley took great delight in preparing tunes to go with the family hymns, but 'Hereford' only became popular through its use in early BBC religious broadcasts conducted by Walford Davies. Through words and tune that match perfectly, 'O thou who camest from above' has found a lasting place in the hearts of Christians, ancient and modern.

On a hill far away stood an old rugged cross

(THE OLD RUGGED CROSS)

Words by George Bennard (1873–1958)

Tune: 'The Old Rugged Cross' by George Bennard

10

When Thora Hird was presenting her hymn-request programme, *Praise Be!*, she might well have begun one of her introductions to 'The Old Rugged Cross' with: 'Hands up all of you who first heard this hymn in church? Not many, I'll be bound. Now, hands up who first heard it sung by Roy Rogers? Oh yes! Lots of hands!'

Roy Rogers was a Hollywood star, the hero of the Saturday matinee, once described as 'shy, drawling and courteous'. He had a pleasant tenor voice and a Christian disposition, and his weekly radio series ensured that a revivalist hymn, popular before the First World War in the USA, made a return visit to Britain in the 1950s. Although the hymn, 'The Old Rugged Cross', was recorded and made famous by Pat Boone, many older film and radio buffs may also remember the song with its clip-clop musical accompaniment as Roy Rogers set off into the sunset on his faithful horse, Trigger.

For many, it brings back grateful memories of the work of the Salvation Army. 'They were always there for the service personnel in the war with tea and soup, no matter how dangerous the circumstances,' said a viewer recently, also remembering the nights in the pub when everyone sang the hymn as *The War Cry* and the collecting box went round.

George Bennard, who wrote both words and tune, was himself an American Salvation Army Officer who later became a Methodist minister based in Michigan. The chorus gives the hymn the title by which it is best known: 'The Old Rugged Cross'.

Over seventeen years of presenting *Praise Be!*, Thora read out thousands of requests for hymns, but by far the most abundant were the letters asking for 'The Old Rugged Cross'. Sometimes, the request was for 'The Old Wooden Cross'. The letters would pour in every year, and usually included stories of hearing it sung at different times and places, often as a solo. One remembered playing with her hoop many years before, and hearing it wafting out of a little mission hall.

> On a hill far away stood an old rugged cross,
>   the emblem of suffering and shame;
> and I love that old cross where the dearest
>   and best
>   for a world of lost sinners was slain.
>
> *So I'll cherish the old rugged cross*
>   *till my trophies at last I lay down;*
> *I will cling to the old rugged cross*
>   *and exchange it some day for a crown.*
>
> O, the old rugged cross, so despised by the world,
>   has a wondrous attraction for me;
> for the dear Lamb of God left his glory above
>   to bear it to dark Calvary.
>
> In the old rugged cross, stained with blood so
>   divine,
>   a wondrous beauty I see;
> for 'twas on that old cross Jesus suffered and died
>   to pardon and sanctify me.
>
> To the old rugged cross I will ever be true,
>   its shame and reproach gladly bear;
> then he'll call me some day to my home far away,
>   when his glory for ever I'll share.

Another had crossed the Atlantic from Britain to America by sea, and after catching a glimpse of Mae West in New York, had heard the hymn on a car radio. One lady remembered singing it around the piano at a holiday guest house. Another described it as the remedy that always brought a relative out of depression. Someone remembered hearing the hymn sung by an elderly fisherman on the now-vanished pier of Thora's own home town, Morecambe. 'It always brings my mother's dear face to my mind when I hear it,' said a regular viewer, while another remembered her father

whistling the tune as he shaved, and always adding the line, 'My cross is very rugged.'

A well-known Christian musician, who should perhaps remain nameless rather than face the wrath of the hymn's many supporters, finds it woolly and sentimental: 'The cross is to be honoured, not fossilised.' It fell to another distinguished musician, David Wright, formerly choirmaster and now organist at 'The Stump', the nickname of Boston parish church in Lincolnshire, to cope with the first request for the hymn on *Songs of Praise* after interviews had been introduced in the late 1970s. Ivan Walden, who at that

time worked close to the great church as he set up Boston's huge market every week, chose it to remember a friend called Poggy, who had asked for it at his funeral. Wright visibly blanched when the choice was discussed, but in the best tradition of Anglican Church musicians, he set to energetically, and the hymn, sung with feeling one hot summer's night in Boston, made it onto one of the *Songs of Praise* LPs.

The hymn is as good a sign-off as Roy Rogers's regular ending to his radio show: 'Goodbye, good luck, and may the good Lord take a likin' to ya.'

Onward, Christian soldiers

Words by Sabine Baring-Gould (1834–1924)

Tune: 'St Gertrude' by Arthur Sullivan (1842–1900)

Just off the M1 in West Yorkshire, travellers pass an unusual road sign: 'Welcome to the home of "Onward, Christian soldiers".' The road has dipped down into the valley of the River Calder, which froths its way across a weir and past old factories, close to a handsome bridge which gives the village of Horbury Bridge its name. Ahead is a long, steep, winding road leading to the town of Horbury, which is topped by the distinctive spire of the parish church.

Hymn detectives stop here, for they are as close as it is possible to be to the nineteenth-century world of 'Onward, Christian soldiers' and its writer, the Reverend Sabine Baring-Gould. In 1864, Baring-Gould, the new

curate, arrived at the 'Brigg', as Horbury Bridge was known. He came from the privileged world of Clare College, Cambridge, and was from an aristocratic family in Devon. Although aged thirty, he still enjoyed a prank, as his boss, Canon Sharp, the vicar of Horbury, soon discovered when his white kitten was turned pink.

Baring-Gould was given the formidable task of starting a mission church in the 'Brigg'. In a house on a little terrace, which today is the post office, he began to hold Sunday services in an upstairs bedroom. It was a tough community, wedged between the vast sidings of the Lancashire and Yorkshire Railway and a canal; within living memory, there had been violent weavers'

Onward, Christian soldiers,
　marching as to war,
with the cross of Jesus
　going on before.
Christ the royal Master
　leads against the foe;
forward into battle,
　see, his banner go!

Onward, Christian soldiers,
　marching as to war,
with the cross of Jesus
　going on before.

Like a mighty army
　moves the Church of God;
brothers, we are treading
　where the saints have trod;
we are not divided,
　all one body we,
one in hope and doctrine,
　one in charity.

Crowns and thrones may perish,
　kingdoms rise and wane,
but the Church of Jesus
　constant will remain;
gates of hell can never
　'gainst that Church prevail;
we have Christ's own promise,
　and that cannot fail.

Onward, then, ye people,
　join our happy throng,
blend with ours your voices
　in the triumph song;
glory, laud and honour
　unto Christ the King;
this through countless ages
　men and angels sing.

riots that had spilled over into the village. 'Even the dissenters neglect these people,' recorded one observer.

Horbury, like many other northern towns, used to celebrate Whitsun with a feast, and it was the custom for children from the Sunday schools to walk to church for a special service. In 1820, nearly 3,000 children with more than 400 teachers were reported to have marched to just one Leeds church. The prospect of persuading the children to march up the steep, mile-long hill from the 'Brigg' into the town on Whit Tuesday was daunting. Baring-Gould had a great number to lead, due to the increasing popularity of his services. People had overflowed down the stairs from the bedroom, and Baring-Gould preached standing on a stool in front of a mantelpiece complete with cross and candlesticks.

On the eve of Whitsun 1865, Baring-Gould decided he would have to write a hymn for the procession. 'You best be sharp about it,' said a doubtful parishioner, 'for this is Saturday and there will shortly be no printing done.' The curate recorded the process in a letter, which is still preserved in Horbury: 'I sat down and knocked off the hymn in about ten minutes. We got it printed and practised, and it was sung to the tune of "Haydn" on Tuesday.'

Thus, one of the most famous hymns of all time was born, but not to the tune most people would describe as the 'old' tune. In 1865, the children did not march up the hill to Arthur Sullivan's 'St Gertrude', as

The Calder Valley near Horbury 'Brigg'.

this familiar tune was not written until 1871. 'St Gertrude' is the tune the present Bishop of Wakefield, Nigel McCulloch, recalls singing while climbing the hill to Horbury singing a few years ago: 'We'd sung the whole hymn through about nine times before we arrived, somewhat breathlessly, at the parish church. But it was fun.'

'St Gertrude' is a good marching tune, although the Welsh tune 'Rachie', most appropriately used on the *Songs of Praise* tribute to the late Harry Secombe, would have had the children jogging, if not running, up the hill!

So, what was the tune 'Haydn'? One biographer claimed it to be the slow movement of Haydn's symphony number 15. Musical experts say that this is absurd, as the tune does not fit the words, but on further research they have discovered an 1810 edition of Haydn's symphonies in which the listed number 15 is now number 94, the well-known *Surprise* symphony, which does fit the words.

It would be fascinating to arrange the well-known 'Haydn' tune to Baring-Gould's 'knocked-off-in-ten-minutes' hymn words. Like the recently refurbished mission church in the 'Brigg', where the original wooden cross that headed the Sunday-school procession is still cherished, the tune that inspired of Horbury Bridge's most famous curate deserves a fresh look.

Praise, my soul, the King of heaven

Words by Henry Francis Lyte (1793–1847) (based on Psalm 103)

Tune: 'Praise, My Soul' by John Goss (1800–80)

21

In an English county that is dotted with beautiful churches, St Mary and All Saints at Fotheringhay is an absolute gem. On the eastern edge of Northamptonshire, the traveller escaping from the busy Great North Road is suddenly confronted with the church's octagonal lantern tower and delicate tracery. The tower sits on a solid four-square base and is attached to a nave supported by elegant flying buttresses. The building, with its honey-coloured stone, exudes light, grandeur and grace, and in any other country it might be expected to be a world-heritage site. Here, it is one of five churches in the united benefice of Cotterstock, Fotheringhay, Tansor, Warmington and Southwick, and the place of worship for a small village of 100 souls. Just one priest, Brian Rogers, serves all five parishes, and the electoral roll of the church of St Mary and All Saints lists only a tiny, if dedicated, membership to pay the bills.

Yet kings and queens of England once came here in great processions. Across the road from the church stood the great castle of Fotheringhay, birthplace of the notorious King Richard III, the last monarch to die in battle. Today the site is marked by grassy mounds. And nothing now survives of the Great Hall at Fotheringhay Castle, where Mary Queen of Scots was beheaded on the orders of Queen Elizabeth I in 1587.

The highs and lows of Fotheringhay's history echo the most dramatic moments in the history of the English Church. The original collegiate church, through which ancient plainsong once echoed, was pulled apart at the order of Henry VIII after his break with the pope. When Elizabeth I visited the church in 1566, she was appalled to find that the tombs of two previous dukes

*The church of St Mary and
All Saints at Fotheringhay.*

of York, who had died in battle (one at Agincourt), had been desecrated. Her orders that things be put right helped put the church into the form we can see now.

In Elizabeth I's time, it was not hymns that congregations loved to sing there, but psalms, in the metrical or paraphrased form introduced by the

> Praise, my soul, the King of heaven,
>   to his feet thy tribute bring.
> Ransomed, healed, restored, forgiven,
>   who like me his praise should sing?
>   Praise him! Praise him!
>   Praise him! Praise him!
>   Praise the everlasting King!
>
> Praise him for his grace and favour
>   to our fathers in distress;
> praise him still the same for ever,
>   slow to chide, and swift to bless.
>   Praise him! Praise him!
>   Praise him! Praise him!
>   Glorious in his faithfulness.
>
> Father-like he tends and spares us;
>   well our feeble frame he knows;
> in his hands he gently bears us,
>   rescues us from all our foes.
>   Praise him! Praise him!
>   Praise him! Praise him!
>   Widely as his mercy flows.
>
> Angels help us to adore him;
>   ye behold him face to face;
> sun and moon bow down before him,
>   dwellers all in time and space.
>   Praise him! Praise him!
>   Praise him! Praise him!
>   Praise with us the God of grace.

reformers. The 'Genevan Jiggs' as they were called were often sung at huge gatherings – sixteenth-century forerunners of Greenbelt and Spring Harvest.

It is a Victorian paraphrase of a psalm that has won today's royal approval. 'Praise, my soul, the King of heaven' is the title of Henry Francis Lyte's poetic interpretation of Psalm 103, and it first appeared in his 1834 publication, *The Spirit of the Psalms*. Towards the end of his life, Lyte was to write 'Abide with me', and like that hymn, 'Praise, my soul, the King of heaven' only took off when it was sung to a popular tune. John Goss's music goes hand in hand with Lyte's words, and the hymn is sometimes described as the 'national hymn of thanksgiving'. In 1947, when Elizabeth (soon to be Queen) and Philip Mountbatten included it in their wedding service at Westminster Abbey, they helped to put Lyte's paraphrase high among the nation's favourite hymns. It had already been sung at Elizabeth's parents' wedding, and at numerous other royal events, including the service of thanksgiving for George V's recovery from illness in 1928.

Today, 'Praise, my soul, the King of heaven' is more likely to appear in Fotheringhay's monthly choral communion service than at weddings, the community is so small. Brian Rogers chooses the hymns himself, and is fortunate to have Julia Abramson, director of the Cambridge summer music festival, as a parishioner. Abramson comes to play the beautiful new two-manual tracker organ.

The golden jubilee celebrations for Elizabeth II included, as well as Lyte's hymn, the first modern performance of some music that was written before Elizabeth I's time – by a chantry priest in the great pre-Reformation collegiate church of St Mary and All Saints in Fotheringhay. History has come full circle.

Praise to the Holiest in the height

Words by John Henry Newman (1801–90) (from *The Dream of Gerontius*)
Tune: 'Gerontius' by John Bacchus Dykes (1823–76)

23

Praise to the Holiest in the height,
　and in the depth be praise,
in all his words most wonderful,
　most sure in all his ways.

O loving wisdom of our God!
　When all was sin and shame,
a second Adam to the fight
　and to the rescue came.

O wisest love! that flesh and blood,
　which did in Adam fail,
should strive afresh against the foe,
　should strive and should prevail;

and that a higher gift than grace
　should flesh and blood refine:
God's presence and his very self
　and essence all-divine.

O generous love! that he who smote
　in Man for man the foe,
the double agony in Man
　for man should undergo;

and in the garden secretly,
　and on the cross on high,
should teach his brethren, and inspire
　to suffer and to die.

Praise to the Holiest in the height,
　and in the depth be praise,
in all his words most wonderful,
　most sure in all his ways.

John Reith, the BBC's first director general and an icon of austere Presbyterianism, took great pleasure, when describing his upbringing in the Free Church in Glasgow, in revealing that a portrait of John Henry Newman hung in pride of place in the college church manse. And yet the fact that the Roman Catholic cardinal's frail physique presided over a home whose first loyalties lay with Luther and Calvin is not really such a surprise. Newman had been brought up with what he called 'Bible religion', albeit in the Church of England, and he was so greatly impressed by the writing of Thomas Scott, a famous evangelical, that 'humanly speaking, I almost owe my soul to him'.

Newman knew from an early age that he wanted to go into the church. In 1819, he wrote in his diary:

Bells pealing. The pleasure of hearing them. It leads the mind to a longing after something, I know not what. It does not bring past years to remembrance. It does not bring anything. What does it do? We have a kind of longing after something dear to us.

John Henry Newman.

Newman went on to combine academic life in Oxford with a curacy in a Church of England country parish. While he was vicar of St Mary's, the university church in Oxford, he delivered sermons that had an immediate and profound effect on religious thinking in Britain. He was part of the Oxford movement, a movement to restore Catholic orthodoxy to the teaching of the Anglican Church, but his Anglo-Catholic ideas were eventually to lead him, and many of his followers, out of the Church of England. By 1845, he had been received into the Roman Catholic Church.

Although physically weak, with a rather feeble voice, Newman was intellectually tough. He had left his wistful thoughts on hearing the church bells far behind. His preaching was inspirational, and he stressed that holiness, not comfort, was what mattered in life. He wrote, 'The Catholic Church in her human aspect is but a discipline of the affections and passions. She is the poet of her children; full of music to soothe the sad and control the wayward… her very being is poetry.'

Newman enjoyed playing the violin, and music often inspired his ideas. On 17 January 1862, he wrote, 'It came into my head to write a poem and I wrote on till it was finished on small bits of paper.' The poem, 'The Dream of Gerontius', was his masterpiece. In it Gerontius, an old and dying priest, dreams of the journey of his soul towards God. The poem ends with Gerontius at the threshold of judgment. A triumphant choir of angelicals comes to bear him onwards, singing 'Praise to the Holiest in the height.'

The setting of seven of the poem's verses as a hymn first appeared in 1868, and with the help of the tune 'Gerontius' by John Bacchus Dykes, the angelic choirs were soon replaced by congregations of all persuasions, including the evangelicals among whom Newman had grown up. It even became a favourite of William Gladstone, the Victorian prime minister.

In the summer of 1900, Edward Elgar was completing his oratorio *The Dream of Gerontius*. On 31 May, he sent the score of 'Praise to the Holiest in the height' to his publishers. He wrote, 'By this post comes the great blaze.' It was the 'chorus of angelicals', and it was marvelled at by musicians for its 'monumental architecture'.

On a summer's day in 2001, huge crowds surrounded St Andrew's Roman Catholic cathedral, Glasgow, as the sound of 'Praise to the Holiest in the height' echoed across the River Clyde. The city where John Reith grew up was bidding farewell to its cardinal, Thomas Winning, who had died suddenly. A giant BBC TV screen outside showed the funeral service that was taking place inside the packed cathedral, and allowed people standing on distant street corners to join in the familiar words. The 'choir of angelicals' had come to Glasgow.

John Henry Newman laid the foundations for a hymn that is sung today by millions. They are largely unaware that they are singing a prelude to the moment in the poem when the old priest dies and the angel finally sings:

O happy, suffering soul! for it is safe,
consumed, yet quicken'd, by the glance of God.

The dreaming spires of Oxford.

The day thou gavest, Lord, is ended

Words by John Ellerton (1826–93)

Tune: 'St Clement' by C.C. Scholefield (1839–1904)

3

Once described as one of fifty or so hymns that 'every Englishman knows', 'The day thou gavest, Lord, is ended' will remind many choirs of summer evenings spent on harbour walls, singing this as their big closing number for *Songs of Praise*. The sun may well have long since vanished in the western sky behind storm clouds, some singers may have discreetly crept away before the end of the recording, and the remainder may well be voicing relief that the Lord's day is indeed ending.

Producer Chris Mann once vividly illustrated how, just as 'darkness falls at God's behest' in a Cornish harbour, 'the sun that bids us rest is waking our brethren 'neath the western sky'. Or rather, in Mann's *Songs of Praise*, our brethren 'neath the eastern sky, on the Pacific island of Tonga. Through the magic of

television, choirs in Tonga were shown in the morning sunshine, singing the hymn in unison with Cornish singers at sunset, demonstrating how 'the voice of prayer is never silent' (and the weather in the South Sea Islands is rather balmier).

John Ellerton's hymn was written in 1870 for missionary meetings, to which curious Victorians would come to hear about Christian life in exotic, faraway places. He possibly based it on a set of anonymous creation poems, written a century earlier, called 'Morning', 'Noon' and 'Evening'. 'Evening' begins, 'The day's grown old, the fainting sun has but a little way to run.' The hymn was an immediate success, and Queen Victoria chose it for her diamond jubilee in 1897. For many, the hymn describes the evening of life, and today it is still frequently chosen for funerals. But for her own

departure, Queen Victoria chose another hymn by Ellerton. On the day of her funeral in 1901, 'a very good congregation' (according to the parish magazine) in a little church in Marwood, near Barnstaple, sang Victoria's choice, 'Now the labourer's task is o'er'.

Records of parish life during Victoria's reign reveal how much change was going on in that era, when so many hymns still popular today were written. A few miles from Crewe, where Ellerton was vicar of a church close by the old London and North-Western Railway steelworks, is Latchford, a parish that grew with the industrial revolution. Today, the tower of St James's, Latchford, overlooks a huge roundabout seething with

A magazine illustration of Queen Victoria's jubilee statue at Balmoral.

traffic on the edge of Warrington. When a new vicar, Francis Powell, arrived at St James's in 1899, he launched a parish magazine, which announced that he had found little to his liking. The church building, which was completed in 1829, shortly before Victoria came to the throne, was originally dominated by a three-decker pulpit. Although that had gone by 1899, it seems that the services had somehow grown longer and longer. The elongated morning service involved no fewer than five prayers for the Queen and five repetitions of the Lord's Prayer. 'Surely no sane man supposed this to be intended,' wrote the new vicar, who cleared away 'the error of liturgical redundancy', and introduced his solution: regular choral communion – with hymns.

It seems to have been a whirlwind revolution, not unfamiliar to churches today, and perhaps as unwelcome at first as change always appears to be – especially to audiences when a favourite religious programme is altered. But it cannot have been long before the congregation came to appreciate the opportunity to sing some of the many wonderful new hymns being composed at this time, many of which are *Songs of Praise* 'old favourites' today.

A century later, Powell's beneficial reforms at Latchford survive. Brian Carter, the assistant organist, inherited a large choir when he came to the parish in 1975. Today, the choir, although smaller, is balanced, with equal numbers of sopranos, altos, tenors and basses – the goal of many a church-music director. Carter, a self-taught organist, admits that he is 'not afraid to open up the machine' to support and encourage the congregation when he is accompanying the hymns. Another musical tradition has also grown up at St James's. The Light, a guitar group put together to support young people's services in the 1960s, describe themselves as 'the oldest beat group in Britain', and they are still going strong.

Today, what could easily be mistaken from its exterior as a church absorbed in the past welcomes visitors inside with a sign: 'Wake Up, Stay Alive and Believe'. There are notices about a newly started mothers' and toddlers' group, alongside details of preparations for a confirmation service with candidates from the nearby Young Offenders' Institution. Without evensong, Ellerton's hymn is rarely sung in St James's these days, but the spirit of his words lives on.

The day thou gavest, Lord, is ended,
  the darkness falls at thy behest;
to thee our morning hymns ascended,
  thy praise shall sanctify our rest.

We thank thee that thy Church unsleeping,
  while earth rolls onward into light,
through all the world her watch is keeping,
  and rests not now by day or night.

As o'er each continent and island
  the dawn leads on another day,
the voice of prayer is never silent,
  nor dies the strain of praise away.

The sun that bids us rest is waking
  our brethren 'neath the western sky,
and hour by hour fresh lips are making
  thy wondrous doings heard on high.

So be it, Lord; thy throne shall never,
  like earth's proud empires, pass away;
thy kingdom stands and grows for ever,
  till all thy creatures own thy sway.

The Lord's my Shepherd, I'll not want

Words: Scottish Psalter (1650) (based on Psalm 23)

Tune: 'Crimond' ascribed to Jessie S. Irvine (1836–87)

34

It was chosen for a queen's wedding and one of its lines was written by a king. It is sung to a tune that one minister and musician says no vicar conducting a wedding who values his own life would avoid or alter. Another says the words reflect 'the genius of Presbyterianism – poetry by committee!'

It has been sung at a wedding on ITV 1's *Coronation Street*, and at a funeral on BBC 1's *Monarch of the Glen*. The words, set to different tunes – even on one occasion to the title music of *The Vicar of Dibley* – are sung many times a year on *Songs of Praise*. Psalm 23 has itself been translated into other popular hymns, such as 'The King of Love', 'The God of Love' and 'In heavenly love abiding'. However, while there is a plethora of popular versions, and tunes old and new to sing, the 1650 metrical version of the psalm, 'The Lord's my Shepherd, I'll not want', is only among the nation's favourites when it is sung to the tune 'Crimond'.

'Crimond' itself first appeared in 1859. To say more is to risk being embroiled in an ancient dispute over who was the composer. Most accept that it was written by Jessie Irvine, daughter of the minister of the little Aberdeenshire village of Crimond. In her lifetime, the worship of God was ordered with the strictest reverence. This happened to such an extent that, as the distinguished historian of church music, Millar Patrick, relates, choirs never rehearsed words derived from holy scripture. So they learned the tune using secular words – although in their efforts to avoid blasphemous practices, some decidedly mischievous alterations were sung:

Keep silence, all ye sons of men,
  and hear with reverence due;
the maister has gane oot tae smoke,
  but he'll be back the noo.

In 1601, King James VI came to the General Assembly of the Church of Scotland, just as the Queen did in May 2002. Here he recited his own versions of the psalms at some length. It was recorded that 'it was the joy of all present to hear it', but for some it was an unwelcome change, because earlier versions were known to people 'in ther hart alreadie'. In the battles for new translations, nothing changes.

Whereas most other metrical psalms are found only in the hymn books of the Reformed Church, the 1650 metrical setting of Psalm 23 is now in almost universal use. It involved a long and complicated process, and the revision of an earlier text of 1643. In spite of the civil war being fought in England and Scotland, in which religion was playing a big part,

> The Lord's my Shepherd, I'll not want;
>   he makes me down to lie
> in pastures green; he leadeth me
>   the quiet waters by.
>
> My soul he doth restore again,
>   and me to walk doth make
> within the paths of righteousness,
>   e'en for his own name's sake.
>
> Yea, though I walk through death's dark vale,
>   yet will I fear no ill;
> for thou art with me, and thy rod
>   and staff me comfort still.
>
> My table thou hast furnishèd
>   in presence of my foes;
> my head thou dost with oil anoint,
>   and my cup overflows.
>
> Goodness and mercy all my life
>   shall surely follow me;
> and in God's house for evermore
>   my dwelling-place shall be.

psalm texts travelled backwards and forwards between the two countries. They were distributed to different poets and their revisions were sent on to the members of the various courts of the Presbyterian Church. 'Everyone had a shout!' as John Bell, Scottish hymn-writer and compiler, puts it. Eight different authors were involved in revising Psalm 23 alone, and James VI of Scotland was himself responsible for the line 'shall surely follow me'. As Bell says:

This metrical psalm is the best piece of poetry in the 1650 revision. Some of the others seem like doggerel nowadays. The psalm itself is remarkable too, because in just a few short verses, the whole gamut of human experience is described. It takes the singer on a journey from this world to the next, providing deep resonance for us with our picture of Jesus and his words as recorded in John's Gospel, 'I am the good Shepherd.'

It finds room for two strong images of God, the Host and the Shepherd.

Working in tough urban Scotland as a member of the Iona Community, Bell spends a lot of time with prisoners and prostitutes. 'Psalm 23 is the most popular with the prostitutes,' he says, 'even though they rarely meet a shepherd. The description of God as shepherd means a lot to them, because it combines strength and vulnerability. Here is a judge, hero and warrior to admire, and yet also someone to offer them consolation and strength.'

'The Lord's my Shepherd' remains a universal favourite, whether sung at a royal wedding or funeral or, as one *Songs of Praise* viewer remembered, 'sung by my mother standing at the sink, doing the washing'.

Thine be the glory, risen, conquering Son

Words by Edmond Budry (1854–1932), translated by Richard Hoyle (1875–1939)

Tune: 'Maccabeus' by G.F. Handel (1685–1759)

At Eastertide in 1774, John Wesley was preaching in the Potteries in Staffordshire. It is not clear what hymn he had actually called for, but the large crowd he had gathered started to sing Handel's tune from his opera *Judas Maccabeus*, to the words 'See the conquering hero comes'. First performed in 1746, Handel's opera tells the story from the Apocrypha of the leader of the Jews, Judas Maccabeus, who led an army against the Syrians and restored worship at the Temple in Jerusalem. The opera's premiere coincided with the defeat of the Jacobite rebellion, but Wesley, who had previously said he had 'no time for Handel', seems to have heard the tune for the first time that Easter: 'I know not when I have heard so agreeable a sound.'

John Wesley was no musician. Both he and his brother Charles looked to other people for hymn tunes, but the effect the music of St Paul's Cathedral had on him on the day of his conversion shows that he was a music-lover – just like the millions who watch *Songs of Praise*. Over the last century, many viewers and congregations have, like Wesley, heard Handel's old tune as if for the first time. Now this tune seems inseparable from the triumphant words of Edmond Budry's Easter hymn, 'Thine be the glory, risen, conquering Son'.

Budry, a Swiss pastor, originally wrote the words in French, apparently to console himself after his wife died. '*A toi la gloire*' was published in 1904 for the *YMCA Hymn Book*, and it made such an impression on Richard Hoyle, a young Baptist minister from England, who spoke twelve languages including French, that he translated it into English.

Handel's music has been a big factor in making the hymn so popular. In an edition of *London Life* from around the time that Budry's words were first being heard in English, there is a description of the tune being played on the streets of the capital. On Sunday evenings, marching behind a cross, a brass

> Thine be the glory, risen, conquering Son,
> endless is the victory thou o'er death hast won;
> angels in bright raiment rolled the stone away,
> kept the folded grave-clothes where thy body lay.
>
> *Thine be the glory, risen, conquering Son,*
> *endless is the victory thou o'er death hast won.*
>
> Lo, Jesus meets us, risen from the tomb;
> lovingly he greets us, scatters fear and gloom;
> let the Church with gladness hymns of triumph sing,
> for her Lord now liveth, death hath lost its sting:
>
> No more we doubt thee, glorious Prince of Life;
> life is naught without thee: aid us in our strife;
> make us more than conquerors through thy deathless love;
> bring us safe through Jordan to thy home above:

band and a choir would appear, all dressed in white surplices, rounding up 'stragglers from the highways and byways' and leading them to the church of St Mary at Hill. This pied piper of Edwardian London was Prebendary Wilson Carlile, evangelist and founder of the Church Army.

Before a free supper was served, he attended to the spiritual needs of the poor in his Sunday-evening services at St Mary's – using all the latest scientific gadgets. There was a magic-lantern show on a huge screen and a horn-gramophone on which the earliest recordings of other great preachers were played. Wilson Carlile himself preached and also played the trombone from the pulpit. The themes of his sermons published in the newspapers of the day reveal why the evenings attracted such big crowds. He spoke about 'the heavenly wireless' and 'existence after death'. A microphone was hidden in an imitation wooden Bible

in the pulpit and linked through the National Telephone Company's lines to people's homes – so that 'the sadness of the bedridden, the incurable or the sufferer from contagious disease is enlivened by sacred song and story'.

It was the forerunner of religious broadcasting. A century on, at the beginning of a new millennium, *Songs of Praise* still aims each Sunday, through the musical celebration of faith, to communicate the experience of Easter.

But for a sceptical generation faced with more questions than answers, the task is never simple. The composer Jonathan Harvey was stuck for a whole year between the Good Friday and the Easter Day scenes when composing his 1982 church opera, *Passion and Resurrection*. He could not find a musical expression for the experience of resurrection. Eventually, he was to find the sounds for the scenes of the empty tomb from the experience of Mary. His triumphant ending only emerges very gradually in the final act as the news slowly spreads.

That was my own experience in 1996. Having been responsible for the television coverage during the aftermath of the terrible shooting at Dunblane Primary School, at Easter I went to Lourdes, to St Bernadette's shrine in the Pyrenees. *Songs of Praise* came from Dunblane on that sad Mothering Sunday after the shooting, but then it went to Lourdes. After the most distressing broadcasting of my life, it was a healing experience, like a personal miracle, to find so many lit candles decorated with the *Songs of Praise* logo, saying, 'Remember the children of Dunblane.' When we sang Easter hymns in French and English in the great basilica, Handel's tune uplifted us, and at last Budry's words began to sink in.

Through all the changing scenes of life

Words by Nahum Tate (1652–1715) and Nicholas Brady (1659–1726) *New Version*, 1696 (based on Psalm 34)

Tune: 'Wiltshire' by George Smart (1776–1867)

39

To open a yellowing copy of a book called *A New Version of the Psalms of David Fitted to the Tunes Used in Churches*, by Nicholas Brady and Nahum Tate, is to enter the long-past world of parish churches packed with box pews lined with wainscot panelling. Simply painted boards list the ten commandments Roman numeral by Roman numeral. The pulpit dominates everything; its reading desk is marked by red velvet, relieving a monotonous brown and beige interior.

Tate and Brady's book appeared in 1696, and was in regular use for

more than 150 years. Churchgoers mostly took their own copy to church, although the gentry sometimes locked them into little boxes in their own pews, which they exclusively rented and occupied.

Tate and Brady's hymns were often found at the back of the *Book of Common Prayer*. My own edition of 1821 was priced at six old pence (expensive), and was sold by the Oxford Bible Warehouse. The prayer book itself includes 'A Form of Prayer for the Fifth Day of November', which is subtitled 'Gunpowder Treason' and refers to the 'homilies against rebellion'. These were read in England not only when Bonnie Prince Charlie led an uprising in 1745, but also later, in times of workers' unrest. My old prayer book conjures up an age when news travelled slowly, rumours were rife and social life centred on the parish church, even if the parson was often an absentee. The eighteenth-century equivalent of the 'substitute's bench' was much in use.

Nahum Tate, born in Dublin, was poet laureate to William of Orange. Nicholas Brady, also from Ireland, was chaplain to the king. Their joint efforts to provide words authorised to be sung in worship were summed up by a contemporary thus: 'And ten low words oft creep in one dull line.' The book was also criticised for being 'too gay and fashionable'. It begins with a metrical setting of each psalm (Psalm 23 begins, 'The Lord himself, the mighty Lord, vouchsafes to be my guide') and concludes with 'Hymns, etc.' – just eighteen hymns, together with a list of eight of 'the most usual tunes'. It must have been unexciting, although the hymns do include 'While shepherds

Through all the changing scenes of life,
   in trouble and in joy,
the praises of my God shall still
   my heart and tongue employ.

Of his deliverance I will boast,
   till all that are distressed
from my example comfort take,
   and charm their griefs to rest.

O magnify the Lord with me,
   with me exalt his name;
when in distress to him I called,
   he to my rescue came.

The hosts of God encamp around
   the dwellings of the just;
deliverance he affords to all
   who on his succour trust.

O make but trial of his love;
   experience will decide
how blest are they, and only they,
   who in his truth confide.

Fear him, ye saints, and you will then
   have nothing else to fear;
make you his service your delight,
   your wants shall be his care.

watched their flocks by night' and a hymn still sung on many a Sunday morning, Thomas Ken's 'Awake, my soul'. And there, buried among all their metrical settings of the psalms is Tate and Brady's gem, their one claim to the nation's favourite hymns. It is their version of Psalm 34, 'Through all the changing scenes of life'.

How would this hymn have sounded in the typical country parish church of their own day? Singing was mainly unaccompanied, and a precentor would use a pitch-pipe to set the note. During the eighteenth century, however, the richer churches acquired a west gallery. Here, a small band of musicians would gather to play their own instruments. To have, as one Sussex church did, two flutes, a cello and two violins was a luxury. Later on, the parson of this church put together a choir in the gallery. One member had a very fine voice 'but for his drinking habits'. In another church, the local MP presented nine bassoons to the musicians 'in order that the choir be not heard'.

A revealing glimpse of the sort of service at which 'Through all the changing scenes of life' would have been sung comes from an account given to a Victorian clergyman by an ancient member of his choir, talking about 'the old days':

We sat up in the gallery and I used to count the winders doorin' the sarmon, while Cobbler wiped his clar'net dry wi' a big red handkerchief and the Smith, he tooned his big fiddle. The Passon, he jest kep' on a-preachin' and preachin', and when he done one, how he wiped his spartacles and went on again. The singers and minstrels wrote their own books of music. Hymn books? No, we didn't have no 'ymns. We sang the Psalms, the noo varsion, any of 'em we liked and anywhen we liked too. No, vicar, he didn't care what we sung and told us to bawl out what we pleased, s'long's we di'nt bother him!

The changing scenes of life indeed – after reading that, we must be grateful to George Smart, conductor at Queen Victoria's coronation, who wrote 'Wiltshire', the familiar tune we know today.

To God be the glory

Words by Fanny Crosby (Frances van Alstyne) (1820–1915)

Tune: 'To God Be the Glory' by W.H. Doane (1832–1915)

27

It is evening in a Gloucestershire village in 1953, and although it is bedtime for a seven-year-old boy, he is sitting up, eating a biscuit and enjoying the rare treat of being allowed to hear the radio. The announcer (was it the famous John Snagge?) is saying 'Now we go over to the White City, where Dr Billy Graham is speaking.' Before the American evangelist speaks, every person in the stadium stands to sing Fanny Crosby's hymn, 'To God be the glory'.

And this is how Nigel Swinford, musician and broadcaster, and one of the regular conductors of *Songs of Praise*, remembers the moment when his Christian faith took off:

I know I was only seven, but at that moment I was convinced that this was the way I wanted to go, the Rubicon I wanted to cross. I was converted at the age of seven, listening to the BBC that night.

I knew that I could, like thousands upon thousands of people, almost like the whole country, it seemed to me, move on.

It wasn't all emotion, and it wasn't even a comfortable experience to hear Billy Graham. I've been rereading Martin Luther recently, who said, 'The first duty of a preacher of the gospel is to show a man his sin.' You need to understand the down side to experience the up. That's what you get with Billy Graham and with Moody and Sankey hymns, and it always leads onto the release from sin, the redemption which comes and, I think, sends you onto Cloud Nine.

This year, Swinford has recovered from a serious operation and is back in action with his New English Orchestra – singers and musicians who regularly entertain and inspire audiences around the UK, expressing their Christian faith through their

To God be the glory, great things he hath done!
So loved he the world that he gave us his Son,
who yielded his life in atonement for sin,
and opened the life-gate that all may go in.

Praise the Lord! Praise the Lord! Let the earth hear his voice!
Praise the Lord! Praise the Lord! Let the people rejoice!
O come to the Father, through Jesus the Son;
and give him the glory – great things he hath done!

O perfect redemption, the purchase of blood,
to every believer the promise of God!
The vilest offender who truly believes,
that moment from Jesus a pardon receives.

Great things he hath taught us, great things he hath done,
and great our rejoicing through Jesus the Son;
but purer and higher and greater will be
our wonder, our rapture, when Jesus we see.

wholehearted love of the arts. It is all a far cry from Swinford's roots:

You might think I had an unpromising start, as I was brought up in the Brethren and it was profoundly unmusical. To begin our singing, a little man would blow an equally little whistle to set the note to start us off; always it seemed with the man with the most objectionable voice leading us.

Although anything to do with the arts was out, the preacher was always banging on about the Old Testament tabernacle. He told us that we would have seen curtains of blue, scarlet and purple; blue for heaven, scarlet for the earth, which a painter could mix together to make purple. 'That's Christ,' he said, 'dressed in a purple robe, and he is here for you.' But these sermons caught my imagination and I thought, 'How can I make something of myself out of this?' and in the end, it's been through music.

Sitting in Swinford's den in his home on the hills above Oldham, we are surrounded by organ, computer and piano. And also by an overflowing archive, reflecting his fascination with revivalist music, especially the nineteenth-century partnership of preacher and musician, Dwight L. Moody and Ira D. Sankey; and that other extraordinary American, Fanny Crosby, the blind teacher and hymn-writer with more than 8,000 hymns to her name.

As he looks her up in his much-thumbed copy of *Sacred Songs and Solos* compiled by Sankey, Nigel explains why he thinks 'To God be the glory' is one of Fanny Crosby's best: 'It's typical of a Sankey hymn, full of content, telling you a story so well that you could say it in rhyme, even if you couldn't sing it. There's nothing too florid, but after each verse, there's an easily remembered chorus for you to respond to the story.'

Swinford admires the way so many revivalist hymns picked up on tunes of the day. 'The banner of the Cross', for example, has an echo of the Gilbert and Sullivan police duo, 'We run them in, we run them in,' and the tune for 'There's a royal banner' has more than a hint of Offenbach. 'These arrangements were there to attract people on the streets, and they were entertaining, even humorous. The humour was essential to the plot for the revivalists from the USA. If you missed it, you somehow missed the theology.'

Listening to Swinford singing at the piano, it is impossible not to be infected with his enthusiasm for the mixture of humorous style and serious purpose in all these hymns, like 'To God be the glory' and, equally well known for its use by Billy Graham, 'Blessed assurance, Jesus is mine!' Fanny Crosby's hymns do not tell each Christian what they must do for God, but what God has done for them.

'It is a cause for celebration,' Swinford calls, reaching for the loud pedal on his piano.

What a friend we have in Jesus

Words by Joseph Scriven (1819–86)

Tune: 'What a Friend' ('Converse') by Charles Converse (1852–1918)

6

There cannot be many hymns intended only for the writer's mother that turn up in hymn books all over the world. *Songs of Praise* viewers place such a hymn in the number-six position among their all-time favourites.

Ira D. Sankey claimed to know that Joseph Scriven wrote the words of 'What a friend we have in Jesus' for his mother in 1855, at a time when she was feeling extremely upset. Apparently, he summed up his verses for her with the words, 'Pray without ceasing.' No one knows what had upset her, but the tragedy that later struck her son is well known. Not long before their wedding, the girl who was the love of his life was drowned. He never got over it, although he emigrated from his native Ireland to try to start a new life in Canada.

Nigel Swinford, *Songs of Praise* conductor and fan of Moody and Sankey, remembers how the tune 'Converse' acted like a computer-virus detector at the Brethren meetings he attended in childhood. If the words of a hymn called for by speakers could be fitted to the tune of 'What a friend we have in Jesus', then they were considered to be of sound doctrine. If they did not fit, they were rejected as heresy! The truth was that 'Converse' was one of the only tunes that the man who led their unaccompanied singing knew. Swinford demonstrated for me how it can be made to fit all sorts of hymns, including 'I heard the voice of Jesus say', and that great Moody and Sankey favourite 'Blessed assurance, Jesus is mine!'

The hymn has been described as doggerel by some, but ever since it was first published in a Sankey hymn book, it has been a great favourite and a source of comfort for many. As Thora Hird's *Praise Be!* viewers, during the seventeen years of her popular hymn-request series, often wrote and told her, the words have helped them at times of loneliness and despair.

It is the sort of hymn that may have been sung impromptu in an air-raid shelter during the Second World War blitz, bringing back cheerful memories of the Salvation Army playing and singing it on the street corners in happier days. Thora used to tell how she always sang it when gardening, and on one occasion had looked up to see a row of curious cows looking at her over the fence, obviously enjoying it too.

At Victorian revivalist meetings, it must have sounded intriguing. Hymns would be given out two lines at a time, since so many of the attendees could not read. The whole verse was read to begin with, and then, according to W.Y. Fullerton, the biographer of the great preacher Spurgeon, 'The words came separately and individually with intervals between them, like men who are to assist at a pageant arriving one by one and marching to their post. Then all stand as one and 5,000 or 6,000 voices sing, strangely gently as if wrapt in thought.'

In the 1980s, visiting care homes where the hymn was popular with old people, John Bell, the hymn-writer and compiler, realised that they all too quickly ran out of breath singing 'Converse'. Bell solved the problem with a graceful tune that would reflect the intimate mood between and mother and son, and the hymn's original purpose. This tune was 'Scarlet Ribbons', a popular song about a father and daughter made famous by Harry Belafonte in the 1950s.

The tune for 'Scarlet Ribbons' has earlier origins than the American hit song, and came with Irish emigrants to the USA in the 1890s. The late Harry Secombe sang 'What a friend we have in Jesus' to 'Scarlet Ribbons' in a programme I directed in the 1980s. The location was a quiet reach of the River Test that runs near the Hampshire home of the late Lord Mountbatten of Burma. Even though he became wet through on a drizzly winter's afternoon, Secombe picked up that gentle reflective mood. Even the macho members of the film crew said that it gave them a whole new understanding of the familiar old words.

What a friend we have in Jesus,
  all our sins and griefs to bear!
What a privilege to carry
  everything to God in prayer!
O what peace we often forfeit,
  O what needless pain we bear,
all because we do not carry
  everything to God in prayer!

Have we trials and temptations,
  is there trouble anywhere?
We should never be discouraged:
  take it to the Lord in prayer.
Can we find a friend so faithful
  who will all our sorrows share?
Jesus knows our every weakness:
  take it to the Lord in prayer.

Are we weak and heavy-laden,
  cumbered with a load of care?
Precious Saviour, still our refuge –
  take it to the Lord in prayer.
Do thy friends despise, forsake thee?
  Take it to the Lord in prayer;
in his arms he'll take and shield thee,
  thou wilt find a solace there.

When I survey the wondrous Cross

Words by Isaac Watts (1674–1748)

Tune: 'Rockingham' by Edward Miller (1731–1807), adapted from an older tune

Of more than 500,000 hymns written over the past 300 years, 'When I survey the wondrous Cross', which was published in 1707, received the highest accolade from the Victorian poet, essayist and critic, Matthew Arnold, who called it 'the finest in the English language'. For *Songs of Praise* viewers, the hymn makes the top twenty, and it is often chosen as a 'fine old hymn'.

In fact, at the time of writing, Isaac Watts's composition heralded a revolution in church worship. Watts is said to have complained to his father about the monotony of church worship. His father replied, 'All right, you give us something better!' The result was the very first hymn to allow singers to address God in the first person, but eyebrows were raised. Enoch Watts tried to reassure his brother, writing, 'There is a great need of a piece as vigorous and lively as yours, to quicken and revive the dying devotion of the age to which nothing can afford such assistance as poetry... Yours is

Crucifixion *by Diego Velázquez (1599–1660)*.

the old truth, stripped of its ragged ornaments, and appears younger by ages in a new and fashionable address.'

He could have been joining in a debate of our own time, perhaps about replacing the organist with a praise band. In Watts's day, when the tradition was for metrical psalms set to a mere handful of tunes, did his critics really believe that his innovation of the personal hymn was nothing more than a passing fad?

Watts used the letter of Paul to the Galatians to create a hymn of private devotion, during which the singer's eyes would be on the cross of Christ, through whose suffering he or she might be saved. Watts's Calvinist upbringing meant he saw God as the absolute ruler who had predestined who would or could be saved. That same God's gift of self-sacrifice demanded in return nothing less than 'my soul, my life, my all'.

Watts grew up in a dissenting household in Southampton at the end of the seventeenth century. His father chose to be put in prison rather than sign up to the established religion. By the age of four, Watts was learning Latin, but a local benefactor paid for him to be educated in London, where he spent most of his

life, preaching and writing nearly 600 hymns. Like many famous hymn-writers, he was a sickly person. One biographer described him as unprepossessing, five feet high with a large head made larger with a huge wig. His nose was hooked and he had small piercing eyes. One beautiful woman attracted by his poetry is said to have changed her mind about marriage after she had seen him!

Sung to the tune 'Rockingham', 'When I survey the wondrous Cross' engages the singer more personally, directly and dramatically with the central core of the Christian faith than any other hymn. The tune was published by Edward Miller, a one-time flautist for Handel. Like Watts, Handel was also dissatisfied with the state of eighteenth-century church worship. Gordon Stewart, a regular *Songs of Praise* conductor, describes a recent and, for him, almost uncanny experience as a long, tiring recording ended with 'When I survey the wondrous Cross'. Long after her bedtime, one of 300 young choristers 'sang the whole of the last verse, directly to me. It was just as if she'd written it herself.'

From the hilltop village of Goudhurst in the Weald of Kent, where *Songs of Praise* was recorded a few years ago, chorister Len Pierce travelled to Canterbury Cathedral to be one of the proud recipients of the royal Maundy in the Queen's golden jubilee year. Pierce and his friend Bob Palmer, both in their nineties, are stalwarts in the choir of St Mary's, the village church, and say they have kept their voices in trim by singing Watts's famous words. Cyril Russell, their choirmaster, who began a long career in music by playing the organ for a whole service at the age of thirteen, says that for such a hymn, the choirmaster must help emphasise the words more than the beat of the music.

Once, Archbishop Temple ended a huge service with this hymn. 'Sing it loud, if you believe the last verse,' he said as the congregation stood up, adding, 'but sing it softly, if you want to believe it.'

With one voice, they sang softly.

When I survey the wondrous Cross,
  on which the Prince of glory died,
my richest gain I count but loss,
  and pour contempt on all my pride.

Forbid it, Lord, that I should boast,
  save in the death of Christ my God;
all the vain things that charm me most,
  I sacrifice them to his blood.

See from his head, his hands, his feet,
  sorrow and love flow mingled down;
did e'er such love and sorrow meet,
  or thorns compose so rich a crown?

His dying crimson, like a robe,
  spreads o'er his body on the tree;
then am I dead to all the globe,
  and all the globe is dead to me.

Were the whole realm of nature mine,
  that were an offering far too small;
love so amazing, so divine,
  demands my soul, my life, my all.

Epilogue

Not So Much a Programme...?

Religious programme makers have an unusual responsibility over and above the BBC's charter to inform, educate and entertain. Every viewer who comes to *Songs of Praise* may be given, as the current series producer, Michael Wakelin, says, 'a glimpse of the kingdom of God'. For some viewers, this programme is their service – the only way they feel they can join the Christian community at worship. In a world of many faiths and shades of belief, broadcasting sounds and symbols that are sacred poses many problems. 'The audience tend to know what they don't want, but are less clear about what they do want,' says Hugh Faupel, the editor of *Songs of Praise*. Faupel shares with Wakelin the responsibility of deciding which hymns and worship songs are included.

'Some people might think that we are operating a kind of hymn jukebox,' says Wakelin, 'but while we are listening to our audience, we are also in direct touch with the Christian communities that many of the production team belong to.'

'We always try to introduce new words with a familiar tune, or vice-versa,' says Faupel, 'as we try to provide an opportunity for the audience to hear the full, rich range of Christian music. Sometimes that means we resurrect an old hymn that hasn't been heard for a while. At other times, it is a new worship song that a researcher may have heard in their own church.'

Wakelin is particularly interested in how popular songs cross over from the secular to the sacred. The Reverend Janet Wootton, a Congregational minister and hymn-writer, was at a conference attended by, among others, many profoundly deaf people. Their worship was lead by Lythan Nevard, a minister of the United Reformed Church, who included music from the film *Titanic* in her service. But she did not choose 'Nearer, my God, to thee', which the doomed liner's string quartet legendarily assembled on the deck to play. Instead, she chose the secular love theme, 'My Heart Will Go On', sung by Céline Dion, which is about the love between Jack and Rose, the hero and heroine. In the freezing waters of the Atlantic, Rose, played by Kate Winslet, holds on to the dying Jack, played by Leonardo di Caprio, and promises, 'I'll never let go.' As Nevard reached that line in the song, she signed, instead of the word 'I', the word 'God'.

In the closing moments of the film, Rose, having survived into old age, remembers how thousands of the *Titanic*'s passengers waited in the icy waters for absolution that would never come. Nevard's signing transformed the song into a moment of absolution. It took only one, small, wordless gesture to turn Will Jennings's sentimental song into a profound hymn.

Wootton, who is beginning a three-year stint as moderator of the International Congregational Fellowship, is following her late father as a world traveller. He used to rebuild schools and hospitals after earthquakes. 'I only had to hear the news to know where he'd be going next,' she says. He always carried the old *Songs of Praise* hymn book from the 1920s with him as a devotional aid.

Wootton has always loved singing with people from all around the world. She says that, as well as chorus and worship-song writers, there are talented, creative hymn-writers in every country, and that email helps them to work as a global community.

'Hymns are not just a treasured heritage. There is a huge tide of brilliant new writing. The good thing is that the best are picked up and have a life of their own in worship, without it mattering who the author is. These are the inspiration of people trying to live out God's just reign in a world full of pain and destruction.'

Wootton is another, like so many of the legendary Victorian hymn-writers, to have composed a hymn in minutes. 'Dear Mother God', now published in *Reflecting Praise*, came to her between getting out of a Victoria-line tube train at King's Cross and getting off the escalator at the top. There are just three verses, based on Isaiah 40. Wootton says the gentle rising journey on the moving stairs up from the warm, womb-like tunnel into the daylight inspired her in the middle of the rush-hour crowds.

Ian Bradley of St Andrew's University is the author of many books and newspaper articles about hymns. His considerable postbag reveals that, for many people, hymns are a major part of what defines the sacred for them. But is the search for spiritual experience through hymns the interest of an old and passing generation? Bradley thinks not, and points to Graham Kendrick's 'The Servant King' as classical evangelical hymnody that can stand alongside 'When I survey the wondrous Cross', the work of Isaac Watts.

It has all the same grandeur and fervour. He also thinks the enduring place of 'How Great Thou Art' at the top of the top forty is explained by the fact that it begins with the individual directly experiencing the sacred: 'O Lord my God, when I in awesome wonder consider all the works thy hand hath made.'

The 'church' of the *Songs of Praise* audience is a church at peace, no longer troubled by the passions and theological disputes that marked the lives of the early-Victorian writers like Watts, Cowper, the Wesleys and Newman. The nation's favourite hymns may still define the boundaries of faith, but they no longer act as barriers to belonging. Hymns and inspiration for hymns still come in all sorts of odd places, and awe and wonder emerge in unexpected ways.

Songs of praise look set to outlive us all.

The Top Forty

1. O Lord my God, when I in awesome wonder (*How Great Thou Art*)
2. Dear Lord and Father of mankind
3. The day thou gavest, Lord, is ended
4. Great is thy faithfulness, O God my Father
5. Be still, for the presence of the Lord
6. What a friend we have in Jesus
7. Make me a channel of your peace
8. Love divine, all loves excelling
9. O love that wilt not let me go
10. On a hill far away stood an old rugged cross (*The Old Rugged Cross*)
11. Guide me, O thou great Redeemer
12. And can it be that I should gain
13. All things bright and beautiful
14. Abide with me; fast falls the eventide
15. And did those feet in ancient time (*Jerusalem*)
16. Be thou my vision, O Lord of my heart
17. I, the Lord of sea and sky (*Here I Am, Lord*)
18. Lord, for the years
19. When I survey the wondrous Cross
20. Lord, the light of your love is shining (*Shine, Jesus, Shine*)
21. Praise, my soul, the King of heaven
22. O Jesus, I have promised
23. Praise to the Holiest in the height
24. In heavenly love abiding
25. Just as I am, without one plea
26. Onward, Christian soldiers
27. To God be the glory
28. Lord Jesus Christ (*Living Lord*)
29. Lord of all hopefulness, Lord of all joy
30. My song is love unknown
31. Thine be the glory, risen, conquering Son
32. Amazing grace! how sweet the sound (*Amazing Grace*)
33. Brother, sister, let me serve you
34. The Lord's my Shepherd, I'll not want
35. Eternal Father, strong to save
36. Morning has broken
37. From heaven you came, helpless babe (*The Servant King*)
38. O thou who camest from above
39. Through all the changing scenes of life
40. Come down, O Love Divine

Text acknowledgments

p. 9: 'The light of the morning is breaking' by Howell Elvet Lewis, copyright © the estate of H. Elvet Lewis.

p. 11: 'Daventry Calling' by Alfred Noyes, *BBC Handbook*, 1928. Copyright © Alfred Noyes.

p. 22: 'Be still, for the presence of the Lord' by David J. Evans, copyright © 1986 Thankyou Music. Administered by worshiptogether.com songs excluding UK and Europe, administered by Kingsway Music. tym@kingsway.co.uk. Used by permission.

p. 24: 'Be thou my vision' translated by Mary Byrne and Eleanor Hull, from *The Poem Book of the Gael*, translated by M.E. Byrne and edited by Eleanor Hull. Originally published by Chatto & Windus. Reprinted by permission of the Random House Group Limited. Copyright © the estate of Eleanor Hull.

p. 27: 'Brother, sister, let me serve you' by Richard Gillard, copyright © 1977 Scripture in Song (division of Integrity Music, Inc.), Sovereign Music UK, P.O. Box 356, Leighton Buzzard, LU7 3WP.

p. 32: 'Lord of the heavens, by whose might' (additional verse for 'Eternal Father, strong to save') by Geoff Baskett.

p. 34: 'From heaven you came, helpless babe' ('The Servant King') by Graham Kendrick, copyright © 1983 Thankyou Music. Administered by worshiptogether.com songs excluding UK and Europe, administered by Kingsway Music. tym@kingsway.co.uk. Used by permission.

p. 36: 'Great is thy faithfulness, O God my Father' by Thomas O. Chisholm, copyright © 1923, renewal 1951 Hope Publishing Co. Administered by CopyCare, P.O. Box 77, Hailsham, East Sussex, BN27 3EF, UK. music@copycare.com. Used by permission.

p. 37: prayer reproduced by permission of Trevor Pashley.

p. 40: 'I, the Lord of sea and sky' by Daniel L. Schutte, copyright © 1981 Daniel L. Schutte and New Dawn Music. Published by OCP Publications. All rights reserved. Used with permission.

p. 46: 'Lord, for the years' by Timothy Dudley-Smith, text copyright © Timothy Dudley-Smith in Europe (including UK and Ireland) and in all territories not controlled by Hope Publishing Company.

p. 48: 'Lord Jesus Christ' ('Living Lord') by Patrick Appleford, copyright © 1960 Josef Weinberger Limited. Reproduced by permission of the copyright owners.

p. 51: 'Lord of all hopefulness' by Jan Struther (1901–53), from *Enlarged Songs of Praise* (1931), by permission of Oxford University Press.

p. 52: 'Lord, the light of your love is shining' ('Shine, Jesus, Shine') by Graham Kendrick, copyright © 1987 Make Way Music, P.O. Box 263, Croydon, Surrey CR9 5AP, UK. International copyright secured. All rights reserved. Used with permission.

p. 57: 'Make me a channel of your peace', based on a prayer attributed to St Francis. Dedicated to Mrs Frances Tracy. Copyright © 1967 OCP Publications. All rights reserved. Used with permission.

p. 58: 'Morning has broken' by Eleanor Farjeon, words taken from *The Children's Bells* by Eleanor Farjeon, published by Oxford University Press. Used with permission of David Higham Associates Limited.

p. 64: 'O Lord my God, when I in awesome wonder' ('How Great Thou Art') by Stuart K. Hine, copyright © 1953 Stuart K. Hine/The Stuart Hine Trust. Published by Kingsway Music. (Worldwide excluding North and South America.)

p. 70: 'On a hill far away stood an old rugged cross' ('The Old Rugged Cross') by George Bennard, copyright © 1941 The Rodeheaver Co./Word Music Inc. Administered by CopyCare, P.O. Box 77, Hailsham, East Sussex, BN27 3EF, UK. music@copycare.com. Used by permission.

Picture acknowledgments

AKG Images: pp. 27, 90 (Erich Lessing).

Ann Ronan Picture Library: pp. 17 (bottom), 19, 76.

Art Directors & TRIP Photo Library: pp. 35 (T. Noorits), 49 (H. Rogers), 54–55 (J. Ringland), 56–57 (F. Pirson), 57 (H. Rogers), 62–63 (H. Rogers), 78 (R. Fournier).

Artyclopedia-University of Texas: p. 45.

Andrew Barr: pp. 2–3, 4–5, 8, 10, 12, 13, 25 (top), 66, 68 (drawing by W.K. Morland, from c. 1820), 72, 73, 74, 79, 85.

Corbis Stockmarket: p. 77.

Cotswolds Photo Library: pp. 20–21, 28, 41, 75, 89.

Digital Vision: p. 53.

Duke University, Durham, North Carolina: p. 54.

Hulton Archive: p. 39.

ImageState: pp. 33, 34–35, 44, 81.

Lion Publishing: pp. 1, 14–15, 18, 26–27, 30, 68–69, 84.

Mick Sharp Photography: pp. 3 (© Jean Williamson/Mick Sharp), 25 (bottom, © Jean Williamson/Mick Sharp), 38 (© Mick Sharp), 50 (© Jean Williamson/Mick Sharp), 61 (© Jean Williamson/Mick Sharp), 71 (© Jean Williamson/Mick Sharp).

Nicholas Rous: pp. 29, 43, 47 (bottom), 59, 65, 83, 87.

Topham Picturepoint: pp. 47 (top), 48–49 (Topham/Photri), 63.

Woodfall Wild Images/David Woodfall: pp. 22–23, 37, 67.